The Color of Light

David Geiman

WHALER
BOOKS

Buena Vista, VA

1 3 5 7 9 10 8 6 4 2

Library of Congress Control Number: 2024925913

The Color of Light
David Geiman

p. cm.
1. Poetry: Subjects & Themes—General
2. Fiction: Short Stories (single author)
3. Poetry: Subjects & Themes—Animals & Nature

I. Geiman, David, 1944– II. Title.
ISBN 13: 978-1-966392-00-2 (softcover : alk. paper)

Design and Layout by Karen Bowen

Whaler Books
An imprint of
Mariner Media, Inc.
131 West 21st Street
Buena Vista, VA 24416
Tel: 540-264-0021
www.marinermedia.com

Printed in the United States of America

This book is printed on acid-free paper meeting the requirements of the American Standard for Permanence of Paper for Printed Library Materials.

I want to dedicate this book to the five people who have carried the teaching load of the Geiman Fellows over the years of the program: Brooke, Kim, Julie, Maria, and Paul in Paris.

And with a special thanks to Kitty for all the effort it has taken to get the poems on the pages.

Contents

Novella and Short Stories

Introduction

This volume is a combination of two forms of writing that don't appear in tandem around the literary world as often as they ought to today. Half of the book is a new collection of poems, composed over the past year. The other half is short stories and a novella. Some of the stories were written fifty years ago in Virginia when I first had minor ambitions of being a writer, and the others are current. The novella is a rewrite of an old story set in Sierra Leone where I spent three years in the Peace Corps.

I have a certain nostalgia for those years in Africa and a certain nostalgia for some of the traditions and institutions of the past. In both the poems and the stories, I have written about things I miss. There was a particular charm and grace, a polite formality, breathing room. I know that this was a function of so-called "white privilege," and I know that I won a good spot in the birth lottery that allows me to celebrate the unique adventures that were mine growing up.

In 1985, the poet and writer Audre Lorde wrote an essay titled "Poetry Is Not a Luxury" in which she stated, "…there are no new ideas. There are only new ways of making them felt…"

For me, poetry is a way to express the otherwise inexpressible, a sentiment that has been voiced by others before me, but a sentiment which nonetheless captures what only poetry allows me to discover. Poems are their own tribute to the seriousness of the topic when one is contemplating how life might have been created, or how the brain works when you are asleep in a world of fantasy and endless possibilities.

I find it easier to explore the possible beginnings of the universe or the nature of a god-like being through poetry than through prose. But prose comes with its own blessings, especially prose in the form of short stories. Short stories are the stuff of verbal tales, of the adventures related around the fires at the opening of the cave, of the heroics, of the hunt, of the life of the clan. They, along with poetry, are the basis for all of early writing, and they still retain their appeal.

David Geiman, November 2024

Poetry

Remnolent

Do you ever take a look at the words you use,
        or should, or could?
Or think about the words that don't exist,
but might,
        with a little help?

Like *Remnolent*, which isn't in the dictionary,
        But should be.
It could be a remnant of somnolence,
memory of the last yawn before a burst of energy.
        Or a dark remembrance of a haunting.

Is *Remnolence* the vague sense of a fleeting
fragrance
        of the perfume
of a beautiful woman on a French boulevard?

Or is it just the regretful remembering
of something you did wrong,
        or failed to do?
A soft regret, a muffled guilt?

Or maybe all of the above, a little of each,
    a general-purpose word
to take you back in time
    to recall perhaps,
taking a wrong turn after a short nap
and finding a lovely woman standing on
a Paris street, holding a bloody knife.

The Grand Hotel Lobby

A sense of remembered places,
sometimes real, sometimes not,
    an elusive place as
fictional as the book from which it came.
    A plush carpeted sitting room
with easy chairs or wingbacks,
    where spies sit partially hidden
waiting to follow a mole or a fellow spy,
    with microfilm hidden in a pen,
to a secret drop, on a dank and
    foggy street.

A tiled foyer with a dark mahogany counter,
    keys in a row behind a stern matron.
Dressed in livery, a bell captain at the ready
    to whisk monogrammed leather suitcases
to a suite or a curtained room overlooking
    a tree-lined boulevard.

A doorman to hand you an umbrella,
    or whistle for a taxi to speed you to
a train and the overnight sleeper where
    you will be seduced by one of Hitchcock's
femmes fatales. Or shot by
    a handsome rogue in high-waisted slacks
and a well-pressed shirt.

Palms in pots beside marble pillars,
    flowers changed daily, they
smell of lilies and leather, and
    a hint of sweat and occasional despair.
Table lamps, Chesterfields, and up two steps
    a lobby bar with a row of gleaming bottles
and Manhattans, Tom Collins, and
    Screwdrivers to ease the transition.
to evening and an assignation,
    or to loneliness.

For evening is the best time in the lobby,
    the right time, as guests depart
for dinner and fine wine, decanted,
    to return at midnight for
keys handed to you by the clerk
    behind the desk,
the lights now lower and softer,
    traffic less urgent,
the piano now only an echo
    of old favorites.
Cash and coin counted into the till,
    the back-office typewriter no longer
typing up bills or greetings or demands
    for payment from the late-paying spinster
or absent-minded heir in the twelfth floor
    corner suite.

I don't think this lobby
    exists any longer.
It went away with steam trains
    and Cary Grant. Went the way
of boarding houses, and garter belts,
    black stockings with seams,
the way of travelers checks and
    night porters, and ships crossing
oceans to Europe and the Orient,
    with passengers in evening dress
at captains' tables recounting
    tales of other journeys to
dark and haunted lands.

Wittgenstein's Cat

There is so, so much,
I am not smart enough to understand.
Take Wittgenstein, for example.
My unlearned understanding is this:
If you can't put it into language,
into, accurate, precise words,
you can't define or understand
the world around you.

If you see a black cat,
you have to define both black
and cat.
Is black really "black,"
or is black just an absence of color.
No idea.

Clearly "cat" is not enough to say
about a four-legged vertebrate creature
no larger, say, than fifteen pounds,
with fur, a tail, whiskers, two ears,
retractable claws, and the ability to meow.

For, first of all, cat is the name given to
a large group of animals, and
the domestic cat is:
Eukaryote by domain in the *animal* kingdom.
A *carnivorous, Mammalia, Chordata*

of the Feline family and a genus
    Felis of the subfamilia *felnae,*
ending up as genus *felis* and
    f. catus species.
So we end up with *felis catus*
    or the common pussy cat,
and I won't even begin to go there.

Now that we have that straight…

    We move on to the fact
that some *f. cati,* overfed by overfed
    owners, may weigh more than fifteen pounds,
(fifteen needing no definition, pounds
    a measure of weight, just to keep things moving)
Oh, and some are hairless, are they not,
    so throw that out.
And some don't have tails, although *presumably,*
    (on dangerous ground with that word, but
I'll chance it,) all *f. cati* have whiskers and two ears.

And all of them meow, don't they, or do some not?
    Do some yowl? Does that count?
And purring, is that a requirement?

So, If I don't hear a purr, a meow,
    a yowl, or some other noise, does that
rule out this creature before me as a cat?
    Which brings me to this: Do I really

"see" this supposedly black thing called a cat
        sitting at my feet, silently staring up at me,
tail swishing back and forth,
        with a dead mouse in its mouth?

I'll have to get back to you on that after I take
        out the imaginary litter box in the corner
that smells like cat poop to me.

        So really what do I know? I have yet to define
"black," "see," "dead," "mouse," and "swishing."
        In the meantime, if I had any idea what
"drinking" really means, I'd have a cup (a round
        container with sides in this narrow, specific case
designed to hold—in this case only—a liquid)
        of coffee, a specific *liquid* made by pouring
nearly (what is nearly?) boiling (one hundred
        degrees Celsius)—don't ask—over a ground
roasted bean from a tree that grows in
        a hot place. (No, I don't know how hot.)

In fact I need to get back to you on all of the above
        if I can just define and locate the glass press pot
—again, don't ask—to make this semi-blackish
        liquid which is a collection of hundreds of
chemical compounds and which will
        restore a tiny bit of sanity, whatever that is,
to the morning and give me the energy
        to let the damn cat out and change the litter box.

The Origin of Genius and Unsought Evil

It is known that matter can be neither created nor destroyed,
that we are all comprised of material that has existed forever.
We are made of atoms that were once part of the big bang,
the brightest starburst to ever light the universe.

It is also speculated that there are ten dimensions to the universe,
or maybe eleven, that curl in upon themselves in near infinite
tininess to result in electromagnetism, waves of
vibrating little strings, each inhabiting its own universe,
unseeable, unfathomable, and expressible only in numbers,
tortured formulae more tortuously decanted from the
minds of geniuses.

And these very geniuses: Einstein, Grothendieck, Schrödinger,
Heisenberg, Klein, admit that insight often comes at night,
in dreams, in nightmares, black visions sought or unsought,
unfurling in endless equations, hard digits: the only way
to prove new truths.

Is all this knowledge buried in the atoms of the universe,
in the permanence of matter, in the photonic weight of light?
Do the goddesses of time choose worthy subjects and
sprinkle their borning cells with embryos of knowledge?
Do the concepts incubate until one fine night,
in a dreamscape of light and color, or a hellscape
of fire and noise, a quick peek into the origins of life
is permitted?

Do these goddesses know what they unleash?
Are they mindful that knowledge destroys time, erodes
the past, collapses the future, and bestows god-like knowledge
on creatures incapable of handling it?
For not only do those brilliant flashes in the heads of geniuses
provide a peek at the origins of life, they also unlock the key
to the end of it.

Setting Your Coordinates

When someone I just met
    asks me where I'm from,
and I say, "Metropolitan City,"
    and they ask, "Oh, what part?"
I might be forgiven
    for assuming
this person knows *something*
    about Metropolitan City,

So, when I say,
    "Oh, just south of the
Plaza, Plaza…" And get a blank stare,
I say, "The most famous
    landmark in Metropolitan City,
you know, site of a great flood,
    a great fire, (or a great deal
—before Macy's closed),"

And he says, "No, not with you."
    And I say, "Well, it's just by
big little central park with
    all the fountains."
And he says, "I've heard of park,
    park,"
And I say, "Wrong city, that's in
    another state,"
I wonder why I didn't just
    say Paris.

The Fable of the Bell

There is a tale about a church bell in Santa Fe
    in the Catholic Mission there.
That the bell rang clear and true and
    brighter than any bell in the whole of the west.
That it weighed as much as six men of the time.

Brought from old Mexico by an oxcart pulled by mules
    over mountain passes and through dry valleys,
arroyos and canyons, past Piñon pines and spiked cacti.
    A bell forged in Spain, cast by craftsmen,
craftsmen trained by the Moors: the Arabs and Persians
    who brought the science of Greece through
middle Asia and past the dying days of the
    Holy Roman Empire
To the Iberian Peninsula.

The Moors, who brought silver and silversmithing,
    a new architecture, new cities that
stayed cool in summer and warm in winter,
    at a time when London was but a sty of mud and filth.
These craftsmen forged a bell with silver and even gold,
    silver and gold and plate from the ornaments
of a people of a now besieged city of another land.

    A bell pledged to St. Joseph in the wars of the Moors
in the fourteenth century after Christ.

It was this silver and this gold that made
    the tone of the bell clear and pure,
almost Eastern, suggestive of palm trees, sand,
    and Old Jerusalem.

The fable of the bell also held that it was
    the Templars who brought the Angelus
back from the crusades, taken from the
    Muslims' call to prayer, now to be a
Catholic custom, calls to prayer by the
    ringing of the bell.

But I think not, for there were bells in
    Northern Europe calling the peasants to prayer
long before these days, and the Romans had
    sounded a flat gong, a gong that gradually,
made rounder and rounder, presaged the bell.
    In a world where music and instruments were
proscribed by men of fettered faith, a bell
    could still call the meek to pray.
Must all religions call the faithful to prayer?

    Does the quality of the sound matter?
Does the pure ring of a silver-infused bell
    evoke a deeper joy, call to a blacker heart,
comfort more a saddened soul,
    roll a greater distance over a spring landscape
or a snowbound Christmas eve, an Easter morn?

Perhaps, perhaps there is a brighter note,
    a shimmering reverberation in that silver
that speaks more clearly to the pilgrim
    seeking solace, speaks of comfort and
the potential for a god that cares.

Sunset, Sunrise

I have spoken of this before, that the beauty of a sunset
    has little to do with the sun itself and more to do with clouds.
It is the same with sunrise, though less remarked upon.
    There are more souls awake and attuned to the end of the day,
the fade into night, the release from toil anticipated, as is
    the evening meal, a glass of wine, a return to home.

And so much the better to announce the arrival of night
    with a last great burst of colors, a received reassurance
that the sun will indeed return on the morrow
    and not leave us forever in the dark.

But at sunrise, no matter the clichéd rays that spell release,
    there is a conundrum. Just as the magnificence of a sunset
is dependent upon the clouds, just so is the beauty of sunrise
    dependent upon the ice and water
in the mists over the warming earth or sea,
    and while the clouds at evening may yet linger
to despoil the night, that does not so much concern you.
    It will go unnoticed as you sleep.

At sunrise, however, those clouds, perhaps portending,
    in their bright hues, perturbed weather, roiled seas, or
a windblown forest: those painted clouds may be telling you
    that the best of the day is behind you.

Minor Universe

Soft night erodes into a nautical dawn, and as the deep
black gives way to a tentative grey and softly emerging shapes,
a part of the world awakens to be rescued for a few hours
from an ever-dark universe.

For that is the natural state of the known world.
It is cold, the cold of eternity, pierced only by pinpricks
of equally cold light from dying stars a billion dim light-years away,
whose heat was long ago given up to the rocks and dust of space
or to jagged meteors tumbling purposelessly in the void.

So, when God said, into this void, let there be light,
how did he decide which star to light?
Why this little star, our sun, one of the lesser stars in the universe
of billions of billions of stars born of a gaudy explosion?
Why choose this one; not even a minor player, with a tiny
strung-along planet whose very life would not exist without
its own barren moon and the raging tides of creation?

Why not be the god that lit Alpha Centauri,
Betelgeuse, or Monocerotis? Why not a white-hot giant
and attach a grand and glorious world to it?

Is it possible God is not so great after all, perhaps he's just a minor
semi-potent god, the black sheep of the god family, a weaker
relative, a poor cousin who was down on his luck?

(Sorry to offend, but if Genghis Khan, Tamerlane, and not to
mention Stalin, Hitler, and a whole host of other garden variety
psychopaths couldn't offend, then I don't think a few written
words here will do the trick.)

Maybe the Old Testament got it right that this god,
as befits his token status, is an angry and jealous god:
petty, vengeful, unclear on purpose
and pretty much inept in his effort to populate the earth
with functional humans.

Sometimes you just need to start over, but even that didn't work.
Descendants of the Ark were still of a flawed species.
Perhaps the church is right when it says we are born in sin;
It's how we were designed, moral pieces missing or damaged.

Which makes you wonder if Jesus was too good
to be the son of God,
Just a thoughtful shepherd and a carpenter
who saw through the flaws
of an Old Testament world,
the inadequacy of ten property-based commandments.
who looked beyond our paltry sun
and imagined a more powerful god
in a grander universe, a universe with a god worthy of the name,
where human behavior would be guided by forces as strong
as those that hold an atom together and a penchant for less evil.

Perhaps he measured God and found him wanting.

The Purpose of Music

Supposedly the two biggest motives for a committed crime are
money and sex.
It turns out that the biggest motives for singing are sex and danger.
At least for animals.

Toadfish grunt and hum in search for a mate. I suppose looking
like a toad
when you are a fish, demands additional talent, although, to be fair,
they are somewhat cute.

Mice issue ultrasonic love songs, which is why you can keep them
out of your kitchen with an ultrasonic little electric thing.
I wonder what it does for their sex life.

Humpback whales use sonar and underwater sounds like
geopositional tools
to figure out where they are, to assess friends, and in courtship.
Way ahead of teenage boys on Saturday nights.

Mexican Free Tailed Bats attract and keep mates with sound.
The origin of the blind date.

Antelope squirrels stomp and trill to warn of danger,
while Guinea Pigs whistle for food.

But Killer Whales sing for the heck of it, for their peers on long
journeys, and
Pacific Chorus Frogs have a leader and the chorus, performing as if
for a soundtrack or social media.

And, of course, there are the songbirds, and crickets and cicadas
and katydids and all
of the avian world who brighten the mornings and fill the nights so
that silence hardly
has a chance, in the natural world.

And finally, Buddhists chant, Protestants sing for salvation, and
Catholics sing
to assuage guilt.

Broken Glass

There is the dream you have, a late dream,
middle of the night, when your body has cooled,
    and the hour for dying at some future date
is approaching, when your story will have been written,
    and only its telling will remain.

In the dream you walk on a cracking substance,
something splintered, a bed of acorns or rough-edged stones,
    unsteady and unsettled and you become uneasy,
a vertiginous fear seeps into your marrow.

You will soon have passed in this dreamscape
into a world of dark shadows and the looming unseen,
    and you know that what you cannot see is not
a minor aberration of the natural world,
    but a Hadean evil born of the dark souls of men.

You know now that you are walking on broken glass,
and there is almost no other shattered substance
    that so signifies the breach of trust, the loss of goodness
or the end of safety, as the bashed window, the ruptured
    storefront in an old German city, the crushed
frame of an heirloom photograph.

A glass window is a symbol of a certain level of civility
and good order. In African towns and cities I have known,
in impoverished inner cities of any continent, a glass
window would not last a night. There, there are iron bars
and steel shutters, over-night shut doors and
light-seeking windows.

Thus, you are right to worry when a night of soft dreams
turns to one with the harsh crunch underfoot
of a trusted barrier, the dreadful knowing that
now lost is a certain proof that things were right,
morally contained and unchanging.

Autumn Two

There is a certain inconsiderate vengeance to the first killing frost,
> For it is often a one-night stand, a cold plunge that freezes cells,
Lays waste a garden or the broad leaves of the oak, and then departs,
> Making way for bright sunny days and what might have been.

If you let it, it erases hope, stirs regret, and pulls you
> Into the saddened, shortening days, the long chilling nights.

But with reflection, you should honor this frosty omen
> Of this most honest season of the year.
Autumn does not, like spring, tempt you with a bright clean
> Day of warmth and then plunge you back
Into a cold damp month of wind and bleak rains, sodden landscapes
> Struggling to bury winter's brown beneath the green.

Autumn does not lie to you. In every pointed gesture,
> From the dying leaves to the shorter days,
From the drying air to the encroaching chill of night,
> From the fleeing birds to the dropping seeds,

It is telling you of cold days to come,
> Nights of darkness, mists, and snow.

Do nations have seasons as well? A springtime of hope
    And the birth of new institutions, a summer
Of glory or conquests and battles won,
    Followed by a slide, forewarned if you pay attention to the
signs,
The first chill of repression, the withering of the common good
    And tolerance no longer tolerated. It is likely so.

The first freeze of autumn is telling you to be aware.

Memory Palace

One way to remember things, random facts, stray numbers,
Names or dates,
Is to create a memory palace, an imaginary building
Through which your mind walks,
Attaching objects to words, the opposite of normal language,
Attaching words to objects.

The purpose of the palace, of course, is to fix that image in your brain,
This turning of logic upside down.
This redefinition of reality, the elevation of fantasy.

So what of the cultural implications? Do they restrict what one might remember?
Does a Frenchman create a memory chateau and stroll through
Picturing fresh vegetables or Impressionist paintings
As he tries to seal in place the dates of all of Napoleon's victories?

Does an Englishwoman stride about a country house
Placing objects of treasure looted in colonial days
Onto pedestals themselves looted from Greece or an Indian compound,
Or populate a tapestry with figures, digits, instead of woven image.

What of the Germans, do they walk through their own hilltop castles
Perched above gorge and forest, and think of Goethe
Or the coats of arms of great breweries?

Do they see the faces of philosophers and composers
And tie music to the memory?

This remembering is all fine, but what if one wishes to forget?
Is it possible to back out of the chateau, the fortress, the palace
And remove the remembered object from its spot on the wall,
Its place on the pedestal,
Its cozy ensconcement in a nook or alcove?
To go from room to room erasing memories and cleaning the slate.

I fear it doesn't work that way.
I think that once placed in the palace, the memory can never be
removed,
But perhaps it can fade if one marches back and forth
Across that space putting new images into its place.

The Nature of Light

Some time ago, while walking across a courtyard
    In Berlin, old East Berlin,
I noticed in a window, a lamp, a table lamp, placed,
    As lamps sometimes are, upon a table
In front of a window.
    The lamp, with its yellow shade, spread a soft
And almost golden light on the red walls
    Of the room.
I could only speculate about the purpose of the room,
    But the light called to me,
Made me think of a library, or a club room
    Probably warmed by flames
From a brick-lined fireplace beneath a carved mantle.

I have thought often of that room and that light
    And its drawing power.
There are so many ways to describe light
    And so many emotions to be evoked.
There is the pooling of light, like a liquid with
    A specific gravity sufficient to displace the night.
There is harsh light, unfiltered, electric, or
    Born of the desert, unremitting and deadly.

Light can be cold, fractured, and unspecific,
    A torment to sleepless eyes and a troubled soul.

It may fall beneath a lamppost on a deserted street,
        And by turns be a salvation or the last hope
For a safe return, the heeded rescue.

There may be a point of light, the final beacon
        On the shore just left or the first warning
Of shoals and death.
        Light may flicker, playful and cajoling,
Or bide its time in a bright spark about to
        Burn the forest and the life within.
There is the unrelenting light of the torture cell,
        Or the wax-fed light of a candle
Near the confessional and on the altar.

There is the first light of morning, defined in
        Dawns from nautical to civil and
The last light of the evening, slipping behind
        The curve of the planet.
Reflected light will replace it as will starlight,
        Old light, millions of years slanting through
The dead vacuum of the universe.

In the end all of these descriptions feel inadequate
        For something so essential.
The universe is dark and cold. That is its essential
        Nature, and only the bright sparks of
Burning stars and minor suns afford it any relief
        And the tiny hope of life.

Genesis

I decided one day to try to tie the book of Genesis to science
And the natural history of the earth and the universe.
I would need to cut God some slack. I'd give him a billion
Years or so for each of the days in the Bible, God-time, so to
speak,
Not human-time.

But that wasn't much help. Apparently on the Meyers-Briggs scale,
God is a procrastinator, because, in spite of the billion-year
Handicap and lots of time to sort it out, God seems to have waited
Until the last few minutes before midnight of the last day, indeed,
The last few seconds, to get the assignment done and a lot of
liberty was taken with the dates,
in spite of what appears to have been
A lot of rough drafts, trial and error, and some whoppers of
mistakes.

Like a rock the size of Mars tearing off a chunk of earth and
Leaving a dead-as-a-doornail moon tagging along for the ride,
Not even a nice place to visit at that,
And then another misplaced meteor zipping along and
Whacking the planet once again and killing off most everything
Designed up to that point, except a few bugs.
Who put this guy in charge? Lord help us. At any rate,

Even once the place got straightened out, instead of just putting
A couple of nice people in a nice garden with some fruit and a few
vegetables,
A nice vegetarian, vegan even, existence, right balance of carbs,
No hunting or predation, he misplaces a talking snake and the
Freaking "tree of knowledge." Where did that thing come from?
And why?
What weird books did God read at night? Geez, maybe that's why
It took so long to get the place started to begin with. Late night
reading, The curse of civilization.

But, if you keep reading Genesis, you'll figure it out. God was a
cattleman.
Honest to…you know. It says it right there. Constant reference to
cattle,
Other beasts of the field and some fish and fowl. But big-time on
the bovines.
And that explains the meteor. Another design flaw, artificial pre-
intelligence
Got Certified Angus wrong and came up with Tyrannosaurus Rex.
No choice but to start over from the parched ground up.

Now you know, it was all about beef from the beginning.

Remembered Rituals
(In the tradition of Proust?)

In the afternoon, one takes a cup of tea, perhaps, or a small coffee,
A piece of chocolate, a pinch of mixed nuts, cashews, pistachios,
shelled, of course.
One sighs, an exhalation, half of breathing, an expelling of
oxygen-depleted air,
Like discarding a snippet of thought that has led nowhere—
One needs it to progress but it reveals no truths.

One stands, one sits, one takes a stroll around the outer paths of the
park,
Remarking inwardly on the slope of a path, the evolving color of
the leaves,
The varying gaits of the walkers and the traits of their dogs,
The hesitancy of exchanged greetings, the reluctant nod.

The air, by season, is palpable, oppressive, condensed, enfeebling.
By summer, a threat and a reminder.
In autumn, a freshness, and in spite of the coming cold,
A certain joy of being, a clarity and a nudge to create.

Winter is its own trial, the treachery of ice
And a short commitment to light and limited comfort.
No need to speak of spring, its guaranteed
And unwavering disappointment. One wishes not to die in the
spring.

Perambulations done, self-satisfied, one seeks a novel perhaps,
Or Thucydides for a commentary on the human penchant for
disarray.
Days past there would be an evening paper, a short summary
Of the failings of the citizenry, dispatches read in the
Dimming light of encroaching night. Lamps lit, perhaps a wood-
kindled fire
Beside which sets an armchair, worn in the right places.

A light supper taken, a young red wine to go with the Chevre on
the salad,
A cookie? A small glass of port? A digestive from Armagnac?
Little degustative decisions to mark the daily event.

Before bed, a glance at thermometer, a reading of barometric
pressure,
Possible predictive for the following day. On Sunday wind the
clock,
Draw up the weights to set another week on course,
Tick by measured tick.

Curtains drawn, doors locked, nights' ablutions, settle in, dream or
not.
Tomorrow, the opera? A symphony? A stroll on the boulevard, a
movie?
Depends doesn't it, on the piece of the ritual one chooses to
embrace.

Obligations

Perhaps we don't always wish to admit to our strengths, our
   inherited intelligence,
as it may cause us to then claim our responsibilities, our moral
obligations
to think more clearly, to make better decisions than our fellow
   beings.
Our lens must be finer ground, its facets more highly polished.
We must see.

Facts become no longer, as if they ever were, mere selections from
   the bazaar,
items from the thrift stores of ideas. For tattered paltry homilies
neither serve us well nor do us credit, and credit we must maintain.
The "utterable truth" of the poet is fetched from deep in the mind,
and the words must be spoken or placed upon the page, must be
repeated
in the marketplace, splashed upon a wall, festoon a lamppost.

It is a burden, this gift, a curse of birth, and in places, it dooms us
to the camps of despair or the cold far reaches of Siberia.
For truth is a dangerous commodity, oracles a threat when
the thread of knowledge is thin, and the tattered robe of the tribe is
   torn.

Haydn

There are two portraits of Franz Joseph Haydn, the "Father of the symphony,"
"Father of the string quartet," the man who took the openings to operas,
Those preludial melodies, and transformed them into a new approach to music.

The first portrait, by Thomas Hardy, in the ninety-first year of the eighteenth century
Shows a straight-nosed man with a long patrician face, full lips, clear skin, and bright eyes,
A slight smirk of success, the disdain of an aristocrat.
He is well-dressed, well-wigged. He holds a brown stick, perhaps a baton.
He is sturdy, nearly noble.

The second, and less preferable portrait, is from six years earlier in the century, in the eighty-fifth year, by Christian Ludwig Seehas.
There is still the long face, but now shown less-graced,
With a very large aquiline nose, smaller more pursed lips and a hint of doubt in eyes
Still bright but larger and more widely set beneath thinner brown brows.
There is the hint of a Nixonian noon shadow, but the scars of smallpox are still painted out.
And less disdain is found in his gaze. There is as well an uncertain turning of the head,

A white cravat round the throat, a hint of velvet or rich fur,
uncomfortable comforts,
An arm extending but not at ease.

It is interesting what success can do to a portrait, how it can
ennoble a stare,
Erase the wrinkles of time, the flaws of an etched skin.
Perhaps the true portrait of the Kapellmeister, the Court composer
of the Esterhazy family
Is somewhere in-between, an amalgam of two pasts.
Friend and mentor of Mozart, tutor of Beethoven, older brother of
Michael.
(What a selfish half century to have birthed so much genius.) This
one, short-statured, underfed in youth, perhaps the meager
nourishment reserved itself to feed the waiting genius,
Sustenance in the small bowl of porridge.
The son of a wheelwright and a cook, no descended talent here.

Sent to train in music,
Literally forced to sing for his supper. Ever after, generous but
sharp in business, remembering the forced, unnecessary scarcity of
that childhood. Perhaps this spare, erratic training forced
Invention. From this man came more than a hundred symphonies, a
new, more complex music.

Once unleashed, he could not stop the flood of chords, page after
complicated page of melodies celebrating emotions, Kings, whims.
And fame attracts beauty. This unlovely-looking man marveled that
women were drawn
To his pock-marked countenance. Marveled at the adoration,
respect, tribute.
Sonata, lyrical movements, scherzo, minuet, trio, rondo: all the
gifted accumulations of the centuries; four parts, ordered
progression, structured symphony. Finale.

The Museum of Emotions

There are only two doors to the museum of emotions
and when you enter, you must follow through to the end;
you must not turn back, as frightening as this
prospect might seem upon first contemplation.

Consider this: should you enter through the
dark portal of uncertainty and start down
the poorly lit path to door after door opening
to reveal a continuing maze of more doors,
more decisions to make or not, with only
a dim light to guide you,
and decide to retrace your steps and go back,
you will never encounter the white-cloud,
blue-skyed room with floating angels and
the palm-strung hammocks that invite you
to the meditative and serene, and you will
never wander through a garden of giant flora,
where you finally place yourself correctly
in the biological chain of beings.

And so, you must proceed on the maze,
opening doors beneath bare bulbs
until you reach the still dark stairs and
trusting, you must climb, you must climb,
for the angels await you.

Likewise, should you enter the Edenic garden first,
languish there, or only meander from
garden to sky and angel, meditate and gaze,
you will be possessed of imperfect knowledge,
blank innocence, and no defenses
for the uncertain times that must come.

History

He sits in his kitchen with his almost collie, almost shepherd,
grey-muzzled old dog at his feet,
the dog twitching in dog dreams
of rabbits chased and a few caught.
It is near to sunset, and the low, pink light has rinsed the pasture
where the last cows amble and nod toward the far corner
by a clump of honey-suckled scrappy trees and entwined bushes,
where they will kneel gingerly, then settle their great stomachs
gently to the ground for a night of rest and regurgitative digestion,
nature's miracle.

There is a fire in a cast-iron stove behind his back, just by
the now bricked-over fireplace, and it seethes and hisses
from an uncured piece of oak, its blue-black smoke pipe,
with the silver-handled pesky damper rising to an elbow
before disappearing into the old brick chimney that needs lining
before it catches fire again. It was a near thing last time,
with flames shooting out above the top of the chimney
and the firemen called to admonish him,
but thus, at least it's clean for this season.

He lives alone now and has done for a while.
He had a wife once, before. But he left for England,
and a near continent to fight a war, and she left for her mother's
to avoid one. Now they are both better off.
She has a new husband, if you define new in decades, and children.
He has his dogs and his thoughts.

He misses her sometimes on a cold night, when no number
of quilts made by his grandmother and their grandmothers before
    them
can provide the same warmth and comfort as a warm body.
But they were always ill-matched, the two of them,
she, sturdy, more handsome than pretty; practical, productive,
given to simple questions and straight answers.
He, as ruminative as one of his cows, cursed, he believed,
with a curiosity and an intelligence beyond his ability to support it,
a hunger beyond his means to feed it, a thirst
beyond his ability to slake it.

His mind would wander from the practical and the productive
and the needed thing at hand, wandering turning to wondering
while weeds grew in the garden and fences were left unmended
as he sought to understand Babylonia, the French revolution,
the causes of war, Austria-Hungary, and the duke with an ugly wife.
He felt only lightly tethered by the geography of a small planet.
Clock-ticked, clock-driven time had little meaning to him,
but collected time, history, had all the meaning in the world,
and in that he felt cheated.

The eastern valley where his half-stone house stood,
where his cattle roamed and grazed, where his old dog
sniffed and hunted, where the creek with grassy banks and
beds of inedible watercress flowed slowly from the
five springs in the rippled bowl of land beyond his house,

down to a river headed north, had left nothing but arrowheads
to tell of the days
before the plundering, subjugated, and religion-tainted
immigrants arrived from the old world.

Even, perhaps more so because of the chaos, the damage,
a war-ravaged continent had spoken out to him, the remains
of a thousand-year-old castle on a far hilltop as immediate as
the breastworks above a Normandy beach.
But here there were no castle ruins on far hills,
no mountaintop villages with narrow streets and tiled rooves
and yard-thick walls. Charlemagne had not ruled
over a declining empire one border away,
Napoleon had not at one time marched across the meadow
below the house nor had his troops cut firewood
from the forest at the back of his land.

No prince had ever ridden by on his escape from or to some
challenged land. No crusade had launched from a county up the
    way,
no pope exiled from Rome had set up a new seat in
an old town by a river down near the sea.

There was no five-hundred-year-old Moorish architecture;
the local church was made of wood, and soft wood at that, no
    stone,
and there were no stained-glass windows or flying buttresses
in any town he had seen nearby.

He felt cheated, every day he felt cheated.
He took no comfort in the safety and the isolation of two oceans,
a safety and an isolation purchased at a terrible cost:
the severing of the memory fed by the cathedrals,
the castles, the now-dry moats, the canals, the villages,
the bakers, the waiters, the wines and the long meals and dusty
    paths
leading back two thousand years.

The Midnight Mind

Dead befuddled ancestors loom in dark frames, hung well
upon the deep red walls. Stern brethren staring into indeterminate
space,
stiff-necked, upright in righteousness, unsmiling. One wonders—
How do they procreate? The deep red wall may be the parlor wall
in a house common for the area and for the era and for the owner in
a community of farmers, an owner of land, mildly prosperous,
forced tither, conventional Christian. The house is sturdy,
high ceilinged, a fireplace in every room, stout
brick chimneys punctuate the roofline, the metaled roof.

But the house of midnight and the early hours is not constrained
by the geometry of the post and beam of heartwood pine or
old growth oak, by the shy dimensions of door or window.
Rather, the walls may soar to museum height, may eschew
plaster and lath and embrace silk and damask and moldings
worthy of a great country mansion or a gallery of fine arts.

At times the house may ramble, may sit atop a hill, be peopled by
unknown hordes, have acres under roof, sport galleries and
ballrooms and staircases that lead on and on and climb into
the clouds seeking the knowledge of heaven.

The house may set by the sea, and one may take a boat from
the shore, may lift it up and float it on the waves, carry it past
rapids and rough water, guide it past the shallows.
Small boats become great yachts, for worlds are always expanded,

never circumscribed, as if the sleeping mind seeks permission
to go beyond the quotidian, can sense what the daylight mind
   cannot.

A person may fly at midnight, as can any object that goes
fast enough, gravity only a suggestion, to be invoked at will.
Time itself has no meaning, it may loop upon itself, repeat,
retract, slow to treacle, a sticky miasmatic fog with no escape.

There is no secret entry to the house of midnight,
nothing dependable, foreseeable. All is chance and the rhythms of
sleep.
One confronts one's past in the house of midnight, revolves
in one's present and learns to fear for one's future.

You may kill or be killed in this house, you may make love,
be loved, be shamed, become exalted, dine with kings,
be tortured, float in space, jump from cliffs, and walk naked.

You may return again and again to the house,
you may leave it for a landscape beautiful beyond
earthly reality with colors refined to a purer depth than
normal vision may ever provide in the muddling air of day.

These are the pure colors of the beginning of the
universe, the distillation of pre-life launched into infinity
and you will never encounter them anywhere except
in the world of the midnight mind.

Belief

At long last, near the end of the eighth decade of my life,
I believe I have begun to understand the composition of God.
In the court of human understanding, I can only offer
circumstantial and observed evidence, but,
when no other answer will prevail, that must do.
We can only rely on what we might observe,
what the heavens have revealed, what the fossilized rocks
might hint at, and an objective and reasoned examination
of the world around us.

Someone once wrote a book called *The God of Small Things*,
and that title, most likely by accidental intent,
revealed the incontrovertible notion
that there is no god except the god of small things.
Indeed, God is the smallest of the small things, the protein,
the amino acid, the first messenger ribonucleic acid
that carried the ability to go forth and multiply.
This was the evolutionary workshop, and in it God was born,
in this simple laboratory of chemicals brought to
miniature life through a spark we may now call luck.

Thus was released the god of trial and many errors,
of creeping, probing, hesitant evolution,
of a cell, another cell, competing cells, and
a small pre-creature, no master plan, no six-day week
of hard work, firmaments, oceans, skies, plants,
animals, humans. But a billion-year creep toward
hot swamps, reason-defying creatures on

peripatetic continents, continents
wandering about the surface of the planet
pushing up mountains and draining seas.

It is possibly only by the grace of a wandering meteor
that the god of small things and evolution,
that a thinking life, got a second chance.
There is neither good nor evil intent in evolution,
only the atomic urge to adapt, survive, eat better,
eat more, see further, ravage, prevail.

Likewise, there is neither salvation nor damnation
in our souls, but an aptitude for learning, which,
when not squandered must overreach and
tear apart the secret mystery of an infinite universe.
There is a certain appreciation for the fragile beauty
and the textured landscapes and the unfiltered
light from distant stars, but our curiosity runs deeper,
to the mathematics of all things, and math, being
the handmaiden of God, must serve us, must break
apart our notions of time.

But it is possible that this god's notion of time is
both too fragile and too slow for this small planet,
this billionth of a billionth of a bright spark
in a long-dying universe, and we may settle to
rust and mineral to await another spark and
another existence.

The Trade

If you had never heard a symphony,
had never read a great novel,
had never seen a photograph,
or a magnificent oil painting,
had never been driven in a car,
ridden on a train,
flown in an airplane over sea or land,
never received a letter,
written your thoughts in a journal;
did not know math beyond simple addition,
did not know of science,
had never experienced running water,
flushing toilets, heat that wasn't from a wood fire,
had little or no exposure to money,
did not know of worlds beyond the oceans,
with histories of sufferings thousands of years in the making
and in the happening,
did not know of spreading cities,
celebrated generals, cruel invaders,
cathedrals reaching for love and penance and forgiveness,
nor of arches and viaducts and stunning halls,
of telescopes and sailing ships and the mystery of pi;
if there was no word in your language for
philosopher, psychiatrist, accountant, lawyer, preacher,
but you could live the life of the eastern tribes in the new America
in the eons before the Europeans came,
or the life of the south sea islander,

comfortable in nature, taking only what you need when you need it,
from lakes, seas, the ocean,
a life aligned in its own spiritual realm, a life of told stories and old
legends,
with no need of a universal god or the horrors of organized religion,
would you make the tradeoff, accept this new life,
if the reward, the price for it would be—
that the civilizations of the past five thousand years
would also be held in this Edenic state of basic hunting and
   gathering
and fishing,
a cultural stasis that would escape the famines,
the pogroms, the wars, the plagues, the charlatans, the priests, the
   kings
and the miseries of the collected centuries.
Or has the advance of civilization been worth it?

Bridges

You should not be able to cross a river without paying homage to it.
You should not cross a mountain gorge without recognizing it.
There should be no bridge that does not make a statement.
A concrete bridge, flat, simple guarding walls to keep you
from hurtling into the water or canyon below is an insult to nature.

It is true that such structures are efficient, mostly safe, boringly
utilitarian.
Crossing them makes no statement, carries no commitment.
They are the perfect complement to the hermetically sealed vehicle
you use to speed you from the boxed environment of a house,
to a destination, likely as boxed as the one you left minutes
or hours ago.

But in traveling in this fashion, over these bridges, culverts, flat
    spans,
you have no need to think of the natural world nor of any
of the history of the place and how it was driven by geography,
the geography you now negate, ignore, and toss aside, forgetting
that how you now live may well have been ordained by these rivers
    and valleys.

The very borders of countries are defined by rivers, armies
have been stopped by them, civilizations have depended upon
    them.
To cross the Mississippi and ignore it is akin
to crossing the Grand Canyon and not looking down.
The very existence of the Mississippi is the clue to all that it drains.

Cities have been cultivated due to their proximity to rivers.
Entire civilizations have been determined
by the water flowing through them.
Without the Tigris and Euphrates there would have been no
Mesopotamia.
There is no Egypt without the Nile, a different Paris without the
    Seine,
perhaps no London without the Thames, no Stratford with no
    Avon.

Likewise and sadly, we have deadened the landscape with our
    shaped motorways.
The fall line between the Piedmont and the coastal plains of the east
has been obscured by the intersections, interchanges, and merges
of interstate highways, city streets, and dilapidated country roads.
The Blue Ridge is just a set of hills now, not a real mountain.

The countryside has become a setting to be viewed through a
    passing windshield,
a distance to be covered as fast as possible, an inconvenience.
The peoples of the two American coasts refer to all the rest as
"fly-over land,"
those eastern mountains that once cradled a benign civilization,
the plains that pasture the cattle
and grow the wheat for bread,
the mountains that determine weather, all of it,
a distance to be got beyond.

Once in every young life, a person should have to walk a significant part
of every geographic element of the country, should have to climb a mountain,
ford a stream, trek across a barren desert, make their way through
an untracked forest, remember what it must have taken to go there
   the first time
for the first man and woman, the first tribes, the first souls to settle.

Clearing Woods

I remember a story my grandfather told me when I was quite young.
It involved a spring, a freshwater spring on a neighboring farm
and a woodlot on a neighboring farm miles away.

Every farmhouse in the valley, in the time of settlement and
soon to be prosperous farms and large houses, had been built
close to a spring, or on a creek, or usually, both.
The spring provided water for the house, the barn, and eventually,
for the bathrooms of a later century.

The creek or the stream provided water for the pastured cattle,
the milk cows, sometimes sheep, the broad-backed workhorses.
Never pigs, who would ruin the stream banks, and the stream itself
with their aggressive noses, who would muddy and befoul the water.
Chickens never went to the creek; a fox or hawk
might take them for a feathery lunch or afternoon snack.

Once for Easter we got baby ducklings, who eventually grew
beyond the hen yard, and terrifying their Rhode Island Red foster
mother,
climbed into the water bowl to drink and swim. Peregrenacious
by nature, the ducks found their way to the creek and ate their way
through a mile of watercress, beyond a junction of two more streams
to a neighbor's pond where we were called to retrieve them.

We were fortunate to have good neighbors there,
with a suppressed instinct to shoot a wayward bird.

In addition to the spring, every farm had a woodlot,
a small forest on the furthest hill, old oaks and pines
to be cut for fence boards and barn repairs and new sheds
and firewood for winter stoves and the butchering fires.

There was a basic understanding of the link between forest and
   spring;
that the water in the spring had to have a source and that the source
was the ground beneath the trees, where rainfall could soak
into the leaf-mulched soil and percolate past root and stone
to a subterranean rivulet that fed the springs on the valley floor.
But I don't think that anyone understood how directly linked
each spring could be to an old growth forest miles away.

On one occasion, a farmer desiring more cropland
cut down his forest plot, tore out the roots and the bushes
and planted the virgin land to water hungry crops
like corn and hay and grains. And down the hill,
suddenly the spring on the neighbor's farm
no longer trickled up on beds of cleansing rock or
the thick slab of limestone where metal milk cans used to cool
in the carefully laid-up stone springhouse.

It was seen as an amusing sign of progress by my grandfather,
an unpredictable inconvenience, an event that carried
a meaning, an event worth relating, but an event with
too narrow a history to be understood as relating to the wider world.

But the story has stuck with me for almost three quarters
of a century. I am reminded of it weekly by some condition
reported in the news, with causes either unclear or far removed,
and I still look at the crumbling springhouses by the creek
in the meadow near the house where I grew up
and feel a sense of regret for waters no longer flowing and for
  lessons unlearned.

The Watchman

More than twenty-five years ago, or a quarter of a century,
the writing of which makes it sound much further back in time,
there was a night watchman.
The very phrase, the title, of night watchman, carries with it
a colorful range of visceral responses,
from the darkest, most fearful, evoking spy-craft and wartime
   intrigue,
dark London nights with eye-blinding fog
or the back alleys of an exotic Eastern city where the air smells
of opium dens and rotting fish,
to a bearded old man with a whale-oil lamp held high
to guide the weary traveler to the inn with warm lights
or to welcome the newly dead and righteous soul to heaven.

But this night watchman was neither nether-worldly
nor spiritually engaged. Rather his job was to secure the farm gates,
to see that the animals had food and water and fresh air
as night set, to discourage thieves and vandals,
to provide security, which is well and truly what all night watchmen
   do.
His job was also to aid the farmer at dusk in planting season,
to bring the seeds, the fuel, a part to mend a broken machine.

On this spring evening, the evening a quarter of a century ago,
having brought the wagon with the soybean seeds to the farmer
who wished to finish planting into night in a race with

the approaching rain, the night watchman
returned to the buildings with the sleeping animals,
satisfied himself in their security and well-being,
drove his battered pickup to the farm gate,
and having locked it, and suddenly feeling faint,
by this locked gate, his heart decided that it would now
give over his job to another, to the old bearded man
from the cathedral painting who would now show him
the path forward.

The farmer finished his planting at midnight and
went home from the field, not going by the barns
or the gate or the now dead watchman. He found
him in the morning, and three days later,
the watchman was buried at the small country church
in a red shirt, new bibbed overalls, and sturdy lace up shoes.

Old Route Eleven. The Great Valley Road

Old Route Eleven now ends in Louisiana. It didn't always go that
  far.
The northern end is at the Canadian border in upstate New York.
It is almost seventeen hundred miles long. It wasn't always so.
Nor was it always called Old Route Eleven, or even Route Eleven,
but The Great Valley Road and The Great Wagon Road
and Lee Highway and parts of it The Valley Pike. Maybe
this confused identity is why few songs were ever written about
this road, not like Route Sixty-Six, which angles its way
down into the southwest, collecting or inventing legends
as it rolls out across grassy hills and desert dry flatlands.

Giving roads names imbues them with a sense of history
or of glamour and adventure. One thinks of chariots and
  catacombs,
persecuted Christians and fallen empires when the Appian way is
spoken of. The Route Napoleon, struggling north
from the coast of France at Golfe-Juan, through the foothills of the
French Alps,
is no more grand a highway than Route Eleven, but Napoleon
went that way from Elba to Grenoble to fight and pillage another
  day.

Just as the soldiers of Rome and the merchants of a hundred cities;
the invaders, destroyers, builders, seers, priests, and charlatans,
artists, musicians, necromancers, and astrologers no doubt trod
  inland

on a dirt and gravel path with the great mountains lurking to the
    east,
so also did the early Native Americans travel north and south with
    their
own mountains on both sides of the road to mark the way.

Then, the European settlers, having populated parts of Pennsylvania
and Maryland, would bring their wagons down this road to
settle in the Valley of Virginia, the Shenandoah Valley,
the immigrants who had claimed the lands west of Philadelphia,
would now claim the hills and valleys and woodlands,
and taxes could now be collected by Lord Beverley for the distant
King.
Sherando, the river that runs through spruces, became
the Shenandoah, and now ran through farms run by German
    Brethren
and Dunkards and other believers in knowledgeable baptism.

Route Eleven was never meant for modern times
and the modern pace of movement across the surface of the land.
It followed then and still does now, the natural flow of the valley,
uphill and down, across streams on narrow concrete bridges
and across little rivers on steel-girdered bridges, themselves set on
abutments of quarried stone, bridges that spoke to a person
as you drove across them, a humming vibration of transferred
    weight
and tons shifted through the physics and triangles of engineers.

The road passed through every town and city on the way,
for what else is a road for? This was before the days of city planners
and town fathers who disliked the in-town traffic and congestion of
articulated tractor trailers, the heavy trucks, and the tourists
passing through to the new vacation lands in the south. And so,
the towns built bypasses, and now you didn't have to see old
Staunton, or make a turn by the college on the hill, but could use
the new straight road or a new looping road, as elsewhere,
to head on down to Florida or the Smoky Mountains
and roadside amusement parks where they would paste a sticker on
your car.

Along the road the motels and the diners and the Burma Shave signs
marked the miles. There was a comfort, an allure to the motor
    hotels,
the new places to spend the nights without having to go into the
    towns
and park the car on a city street and take an elevator to a room
on the fifth floor of a solid brick building that had stood for decades.
It was the beginning of the hollowing out of the hearts of the towns
along the way, the isolation from the communities. Where you
    could
sit in your car and someone would bring your food to you,
attach a tray to your car window and place the burger and fries
and the Cherry Coke or the RC Cola,
the Grapette or the Dr Pepper, on it.
Or you ate at the truck stop, because everyone said that
truckers ate there, so it must be good, forgetting that truckers
ate there, because it was the only place you could park a truck.

Such was the developing wisdom of the times.

Eventually, of course, even the little bypasses could not do the job.
And no one cared if Route 11 passed over Natural Bridge,
down by Lexington, a feature that Thomas Jefferson had surveyed.
The German invention, the motorway, the Interstate Highway
    system
came to be born, and how apt the name, not the *Intercity* highway
system, but the *Interstate* highway system, which could take you
past the troublesome little burghs and boring little towns
with the five and dimes and the soda fountains and stoplights.

Now you could pass through a state, half a nation even,
and never have to consider the culture, the customs,
the churches, the old bank buildings built by once famous
    architects,
the Carnegie libraries or the city halls and county office
buildings where courts met to mete out justice in buildings
that were once the pride of the small town,
the heart of the town square, would never have to read
the plaque, the obelisk with the list of names of the local boys
who died in two wars, or three, more likely,
nor have to pass the National Guard Armory, where
the canvas-covered trucks with knobby tires and the
camouflaged trailers are parked in rows, waiting for the
callup of reservists, or see the hospital with two wings,
one floor, served by a volunteer rescue squad and doctors
from another country, paying back the price of training here.

It takes time to drive on Route 11. The steel girder bridges are gone,
notably the one where the tractor trailer loaded with plate glass
collided head on with the chicken truck one early morning in the
   fog.
There is now a concrete tube under the road and almost
no one remembers who died there or when. And few remember
that just down the road, the ghostly buildings on the hill
once housed a military school, or that just by the road the local
train would stop at the station for mail and a few passengers
and you could smell the dairy cows in the barn just across the
   tracks.

The motor hotels are gone or have turned into sad relics with faded
signs swinging from rusty poles and weeds growing in the parking
   lots.
You stay at the hotels at the exits for the interstate now, and eat at
the dozen or two restaurants that serve the same fast foods
in every state, making this one of the few achievements of
true national unity. And it is said, by the statisticians who count
   these things,
that the further you are from the interstate, the further you are
from prosperity and liberal sharing notions, from the true
notions of a republic. Is this true the world over? Did the highways
drain the countryside and sap the villages, like great rivers or a body
with veins and no arteries? It is trite and commonplace to lament,
but sadness lurks in the empty rooms of the old motels and
loneliness seems to seep from the empty stretches of the old valley
road.

And it feels at times as if the fast highway is our own worst enemy,
a vacuum, an irresistible gravity, like the moon on the oceans,
   drawing
us away to great urban centers and the cities on the coasts.

Afternoon

A light breeze grazes the windowsill and slips into the room,
    Stirring the curtain edges, jostling the late wash of afternoon sun
And shape-shifting the uncommitted shadows on the floor and
    wall.

The air is dryly crisp after the storm and feels as if it has been newly
    Distilled, a fresh new dose of atmosphere tumbled down from
        above,
Pristine, vibrant even, sparkling with possibility.

It's best not to think about the fact that today's fresh air
    Was someone else's muggy, stormy, cloying, particle-infused
Miasma maybe from the south or west just days ago,
    That has had, for now, the moisture, the dust, the heat
Stripped out, and tomorrow will move along still to parts unknown,
    Carrying new dust, old pollen, perhaps a bit of smoke
From a backyard barbecue and fleeting smells from
    Lives, this time, lightly touched.

Summer Lost

We have ruined summers and summer's nights with our cities, with
concrete and high rises, parking lots and big boxy stores.
With square rooms of trapped air, black roofs, and windows
either too large or too small, depending on where we placed them.

We forgot how the air moves on its own, forgot the concept of the
sleeping porch, the screened atelier where even on the hottest of
   nights
a coolness would settle, and where the white noise of nature,
the crickets, cicadas, and tree frogs would calm us.

We abandoned our forest homes and then destroyed them
and locked ourselves in cubicles, isolated from
the meditation of the night, electric fans and chillers
the new authors of a gray-white sound to reassure us.

For every action there is an equal and harmful reaction
in the realm of hot and cold. We only chill by generating heat,
by blighting the sides of buildings with churning blades
compressing gas and making our task yet harder.

Apparently, we passed the tipping point, and the logic of
a less congested way of living no longer seems to be an option.
We are trapped in the great cities and the square rooms,
and the roads to the forests and under the trees are gone.

Titles

I had just returned from A Passage to India,
    where The Sun Also Rises in the east,
and had set out for The Bridge of San Luis Rey
    with The French Lieutenant's Woman,
whose ship had been becalmed in
    The Wide Sargasso Sea, when
The Painted Bird of legend flew by.
    One Flew Over the Cuckoo's Nest
She said to me as we sat down to
    A Naked Lunch at the nudist resort.
Then it was Gone with The Wind.
    She had lovely White Teeth
And breasts like Lolita.
    Let's get to The Heart of the Matter
I said, there is a Pale Fire
    Burning under The Sheltering Sky
Which portends A Death in the Family.
    Oh dear she said, Under the Net
That kept the mosquitoes away,
    The Assistant from Housekeeping
Said we were crossing
    The Tropic of Cancer,
But I have An Appointment in Samarra.

Things Fall Apart when Money
Fails to change hands.
   Do you record it in The Golden Notebook?
I asked, or Play It as It Lays?
   Depends, she said, The Corrections are
Simple, a bit of White Noise helps
   To confuse them. The Light in August
Is so lovely, don't you think?
   All the King's Men couldn't tear me
Away from you, I said. I'd love to have you
   In my Possession. But you are
On The Road too much, she replied.
   I won't feel Beloved. You're
Like The Invisible Man. I wish
   You'd Never Let Me Go.
On the other side of the pool
   Their Eyes Were Watching God
While The Sound and The Fury
   Of a building storm could be heard.

The Prairie

The problem with the prairie is cheap light.
    Not cheap as inexpensive, but cheap, as in 'no class.'
It's easy light, it spreads its rays around for whoever asks,
    You don't have to sidle up and ask it for a date,
Or buy it a drink or take it out to dinner. You can have
    It just for the asking. Unless it's raining of course.

It's there first thing in the morning and the last thing at dusk.
    Even in winter, you don't have to wait for it
To struggle over some mountain or a bunch of hills,
    It doesn't wait till after breakfast to finally grace a deep valley.
It's just there, nowhere to hide, nothing to wait for.
    And you don't have to worry about it slipping away
While you're not looking as dinnertime approaches.

And that's the problem, you see. You don't value things
    That come too easy, that you're always sure of.
In the mountains in the west, you never know when
    The sun will finally show up. By December you
Might wonder if someone forgot to poke another
    Hunk of uranium in the firepit the night before.

So when it finally shows up about nine o'clock,
    Hungover, flat, cool, and indifferent, you forget
about how it left you in the cold the previous evening,
    Walked out without a kiss to warm you through
the night and left you to freeze your sorry ass.
    You are so happy to see it that all is forgiven
And you welcome her, late again, with open arms.

River of Doubt

Down by the river of Doubt, I came across a wanderer.
He could not make up his mind whether or not to cross.
Behind him lay a forest of dark shadows hiding,
thickets of uncertainty, crooked footpaths leading to
destinations where both danger and adventure lurked.
The wanderer had set out on a path in the morning,
only to turn back when a cloud crossed the sun,
which he took to be an omen. A black bird with glossy
feathers taunted him from a tree branch, and he took
the raucous outpouring to be a warning instead of a celebration.

I asked him if the bird might not have been welcoming him
and not warning him. He had not considered that.
Now he was torn, and waves of consternation crossed his brow.
What might I have missed, he asked, what might I have missed?
Is the bird still there, I wonder, he mused.
As we lingered amongst the rocks and sand, river water
pooling and spilling under the midday sun from the tiny ersatz
    beach,
a loon was heard. Loons live in lakes and thus the river
must lead to or lead away from such a lake, a place
of depth and stability and no splashing disturbing currents.

I pointed this out to him.

Do you think I should seek the shore of the lake? He asked.
Did you have a purpose when you set out this morning,
I queried. Just to wander, he said, just to wander a bit.
Did you wish to wander with no purpose or to return with
a tidbit, perhaps, of new knowledge, something geographical,
the name or song of a bird, a glimpse scurrying ground life;
I see you carry no guidebook. No, no, he said, I had no destination,
no set goal. Well, then we are equals met on a path today,
I smiled and said. I have no idea where you are coming from
and you have no idea where you are going,
so any path will suit you well. You may as well seek the lake.

The Iron Curtain

When the Iron Curtain was pulled across the map of Europe,
when the hard fabric of intolerance,
was pulled across the windows and the doorways,
and half a continent turned out the lights
and settled into the darkness of mistrust, informants,
and secret police,
The curtain rods, the valances, and the dark metal hoops
that would hold this heavy curtain were already in place.

The carpenters, the masons, the decorators and installers
had hung other curtains on these borders, had trod on earlier rights,
and in the halls of government and the cold rooms of
old palaces long past days of glory and artistic patronage,
the new rulers, bereft of mercy and distilled now to the lowest
common forms of thought, would now dispense a cruel injustice
and blinker progress and peering intelligence.

More than two-thirds of a continent slipped back in time,
or when fortunate, remained merely stalled in time,
and with looted technology and rusting machines,
developed societies that rewarded the basest of mediocrity
and killed the soul. It turns out that the dictatorship
of the proletariat is no kinder than any other dictatorship.

Is it merely the luck of history that only the English-speaking,
the German-based language people, or those, with one
exception, whose mother tongue was born in Rome,
were spared this fate, had the good fortune to express the
true will of the people and achieve a bland comfort?
Surely one can speak of freedom in Serbian, Polish, Hungarian?

But perhaps after centuries of empire and the dictates
of ever more inbred ruling families, the collective mind,
like a hive of bees, can no more change its mode of existence
than the hive abandon its queen and turn drones into kings.

True Believers All

I woke in the night, just an hour or two past the tolling
of the midnight bells, the cool hours when death comes whispering,
in the land of the true believer, and imagined in the shadows
of the tired and dusty room, that a servant of a different god
waited, and that should I give me permission, he would take me.

I had journeyed to a distant land, neither naïve nor merely innocent,
insufficiently committed to any creed and thus an infidel, and
in the eye of the believer, an empty soul, and an expendable
affront to ignorant mysticism and blind linear belief.

Had I truly woken or was I still in the eye-fluttering realm
where the mind sorts the cacophonous deluge of the daylight hours
onto the balance sheet of reason and precious doubt,
or had I stepped into a private purgatory and might I not wonder
if this purgatory contained more than one door leading away?

I would be lying if I said I had come to this land seeking the truth,
for I doubt there is such a thing. If the urn of the poet is correct and
truth is beauty, and beauty is in the eye of the beholder,
is truth not then also in the mind's eye of the beholder? And is this
   not
the subjectivity that draws the battlelines in the war for god?

I have not told you from whence I came: east or west. You may well
picture a traveler in a white linen suit at dinner, now recently asleep
   in

a high-ceilinged room with a wood-bladed fan turning lightly the
desert air. In the distance the lone bark of a dog or the solitary
braying of a donkey. Perhaps an oasis or the lingering smell of
turmeric or strong coffee brewed in a long-handled pot over coals
come to mind. Date palms swaying and a dust storm on the
　horizon.

I have not spoken of the age, the era, or whether by steamship,
masted clipper, or slow clicking sleeper car over an endless
plain did I travel. Nor whether by airplane, flying boat, or
less salubrious, an ancient bus, prone to flat tires and a hot engine.
Air-conditioned car, a tram, a horse-drawn carriage. Depending
on one's heroes, the choices are endless.

Might I not have arrived in a desert town in a western country,
or stepped down from the last Greyhound bus to Tupelo,
bearded and turbaned, a rolled rug under my arm?

Or might I merely have failed to cross the street,
to not have shown another man's version of respect,
or just possibly, at another time and place, have not
understood that no amount of learning,
courage, achievement, or patronage,
would ever translate,
ever be enough to render my beliefs non-threatening.

Observations on the Weekly Readings

Reclining lazily (how else might one recline—purposefully,
abjectly, remorsefully, gallantly, hedonistically
surrounded by images of nymphs, bare-breasted women
and silver plates laden with red and white grapes?)—
I thought back over the readings, both suggested, and those
actually read, of the past week, and came to conclusions.

There was a traveler who no longer reveled in travel, but who still
traveled,
who bored me with the privileged sense of a bit too much money
and a bit too little curiosity. There was only one possible response—
Why not stay home? Which is what another writer implied
in saying one learns little from the experience or of the people.
Perhaps the old dictum of not shooting the messenger doesn't apply
here.
There was an essay, longer than many a novella,
that spoke of a Phoenix with burned wings
and a desiccated landscape as if it were the model
for the ending of all civilization in the country. Surely,
a nation this diverse can come up with more ways than
pumping an aquifer dry to desecrate a culture?

A literary magazine charmed me with its discussion of decadence,
Dorian Gray as the poster child for indulgence, while failing
to note that decadence might come not just from the suggestive
woodcuts of an Aubrey Beardsley, but from the abandonment
of time to meaningless hours tap, tap, tapping a small screen
and looking for love in mechanical places.

One young mother admonished women to marry young
and have children, many of them, in order to save society,
while another has become the guru to the mothers who
did have children, and now wish to save themselves
and not society, by exploring their sexual options,
by abandoning, if only just lightly, the same norms that Dorian did.

It is all a bit much, sometimes, curiosity. The inability to
not look, to not read. There might be a bit of wisdom, the key
to a chest of treasures not yet found, the answer to a question
not yet asked, the map to a destination not yet planned, advice
for a problem not yet encountered, or the final connection
between the known history of the world and the future history to
    be written.

The Lake

On the winding road that led by the old cattle scales
    In the rich heart of an eastern valley
A large mansion, red-bricked, white-trimmed
    Stretch-winged, stood beyond a lake,
Its image reflected by day in blue-clear water
    Its lights refracted by night.

The lake was a thing of seeming magnificence
    Its shimmering surface a jewel
In a groomed setting of lawn and evergreens.
    On windy days tiny whitecaps meringued
The surface and the lake took on a new life,
    Little waves striking the cat-tailed shore,
Brown-flecked foam seething in the eddies.
    You could imagine schools of fish
Darting about in the churning depths
    Or picture a schooner rounding up
To avoid the shallows of a real ocean beyond.

But one day I drove by, and the lake had been drained
    And it was revealed that this lake was
Nothing more than a shallow mud-based
    Reflecting pond, no more than

A foot deep over a flat brown-gray bottom.
    A heavy rain had torn a breach in the low dam
On the far side of the pond, and now,
    A low trickle of water from an idling stream
Made its way through a dirty channel
    Cut into the mud.

Eventually the dam was repaired and over the weeks
    The pond gradually refilled,
But its magic was gone, and I came to suspect
    Illusions in all of the world around me,
From the daily unanswered, unacknowledged
    Prayers of childhood
To the smile on the face of the gas station attendant
    As he cleaned the windshield of the car.

I came to wonder if all surfaces hid beneath them
    The violence and essential ugliness of their origins,
The heat of a molten planet, the pillages
    Born of the hard human heart.
If all of civilization was held together by the
    Thinnest of threads, or merely a shallow
Bright pool reflecting hope, desire, and trampled love.

The Rails

There is a conundrum provoked in the peripatetic mind
When the traveler scans the railroad tracks crisscrossing
Through the throat of the train station and out,
Disappearing beyond the horizon or around a bend.
On one hand, these ever-parallel alloys of steel,
Visible proof of Euclid's axiom, spiked down to wooden sleepers
Or spring-bolted to concrete, call to adventure,
Conjure up visions of steam and smoke, mournful whistles
In the sad hours of the morning and the last outpost
On the weed-stricken line into the Burmese jungle.

On these rails sped the great trains of the world.
The Orient Express promised the scents and dangers
Of the East, the minarets of Constantinople, the scimitars
And the silken cords that strangled the royal siblings and
Protected the rule of the Ottoman princes in gilded palaces.
Along the way, a cultural history strewn along the tracks
And in the stations of Paris, Lausanne, Milan,
Venice, Zagreb, and Sofia.

The Trans-Siberian Express, the only practical way to cross
The vast and endless bleakness of the Russian plains, on
The same tracks that carried the New Pioneers and
The displaced peasants to a new and deadening future,
Past Lake Baikal, Mongolia and on to Vladivostok,

The beauty of the station names, Yekaterinburg, Novosibirsk,
Krasnoyarsk, Irkutsk, Ulan-Ude, and Khabarovsk, believing
The squalor, the wooden huts, the vodka-soaked lives
And the crushed dreams of dead souls.

There were trains to Tibet, to Victoria Falls, through
The Canadian Rockies, to the French coast and the
English north, across Japan, the width of Australia
And down into Patagonia. To Chicago, Santa Fe, and Los Angeles.

But every journey on every great train is temporarily
An elegant moving imprisonment, a piece of someone else's history.
You will not be the first to go there and the rails themselves
Are a magnificent, seductive confinement to a narrow piece
Of geography, a slice across a country, a continent, a culture
A hermetic inclusion depending on you for release.

Regret

The dissipated ex-colonial lounges on the balcony
Of the once elegant hotel in a sweltering city on the African coast,
Marinating in a gin-induced fugue state of regrets and
    remembrances,
Scrolling down a mental slate of slights, half-remembered drunken
afternoons
And the soft entwinings of native limbs.
He bore the white man's burden on sweat-soaked shoulders and
A then-straight back, extolling the virtues of starched shirts and
Well-creased pants, highly polished boots and a hat worn well.

He thinks now it was all for naught, except the momentary gain of
    trade
And commercial export, and the recruitment of stewards to pour
    your tea,
Foot soldiers to die for your King and your country, and factotums
    for all the rest.
One sallied forth to the pestilential jungles. The temperate zones
    had already
Been settled to a state of religious competition and the whims
Of overreaching tyrants, greedy clergy, and the pillages of emperors.
Only the tropics remained or the occasional Indian hill stations and

Meandering highlands of eastern Africa, this equatorial remainder
    with cultures
To which only indifference must be paid, abandoned, to the
    western eye,
By the renaissance and any enlightenment, and the great library of
Timbuktu of insufficient interest to a Bodleian scholar.
If one were true to the spirit of the burden, one still dressed for
    dinner,
Drank Claret, and sweated the Stilton and the Gloucester before
serving.
You came to a place, saw it not for what it was, but for what
You wished it to be, you subdued it, you governed it, and still it was
ruined.
It was the fault of the locals. You did your best.
Now, from the perch on this balcony, with creaking French doors
Thrown open wide, street noise and gutter smells wafting through,
The former master snaps his fingers at a waiter lurking desultorily
Behind a bar with flaking paint and orders another gin and tonic,
Go generous on the gin.

Time

Time, the one thing you thought constant,
    Isn't. Perversely,
        the faster you move, the slower it does.
But, then again, should this surprise you? Time has always been a
plaything, measured by
    a mishmash of sloppy devices, sun and moon and god-
    dependent.
        Until the French decided twenty-four hours in one day was
        too many,
and made a small clock with twelve numbers,
putting midnight and noon at the top
    thus starting and ending the day at night, a further perversity
it might seem, but also possessed of a certain inarguable logic.
    Before that, time ran helter-skelter about the landscape,
        days starting at noon, days starting at dawn, at dusk, at
        whim.
Now, the ticking clock could collect the seconds into minutes,
    the minutes into hours and the hours into bundles of
        half-dark days and half-light nights. So French.
Of course, the Egyptians had measured time in twelve decans,
    based on groups of constellations, sundial tracked by day;
        by night, the water clock or the angle of the pole star,
            none precise, precision not needed by the slow-flowing
            Nile.

Indeed, precision and constancy were never important
    until trains came. Perhaps that's the downfall of leisure
        and showing up late for work.
No longer would it do for every village, glen, and town
    to possess its own time zone,
        hours announced by the town crier or the church bell.
Trains collide when the eastbound freight meets the westbound
    and the engineers are speeding along in their own time-world.
It is the ultimate example of the time-space continuum
    at a level of misunderstood levity.
        If the two trains meet at the same time in the same space,
           there will be no continuing.
None of which helps me understand how, if I were to launch myself
    across the country at close to the speed of light,
I would arrive hours, days, perhaps even weeks or months,
    after a friend who might choose to take the train.
        Especially given the state of the trains.

Years

Time spools out, turning right around the spindle,
     defining clockwise, hands pointing to numerals
and measured dashes. One minute is six degrees of the circle,
     Ten seconds tick off a single degree.
This is the revolution of time that everyone understands,
     It paces the world, with clock hands climbing
like the sun to the noontime peak, and settling
     slowly into the afternoon, evening, and another
climb to midnight, deep darkness, and the hope that all is well.
     Even digital watches and bright numbers flashing
on a screen cannot obliterate this concept.

But to me, years roll out the other way, around a circle.
     The year is not a flip of a calendar page, nor is it part of a linear
progression, a long time extending from the moment
     of the big bang into a dark future of receding stars
and an exhausted sun or a moon gradually drifting away.
     A year is a distinct disc, that begins at a moment past
midnight on the first day of January and goes left
     against the clock. Thus, January nestles between
eleven and twelve or between north and northwest
     if you prefer, and every day is a degree. Like
the Egyptians, I must distribute the extra five days
     somehow, so I sprinkle them here and there.
Or ignore them. No one is perfect.
     Thus, the year slides down the left side of the disc
warming into Spring and down in the southwest we get

Into May, slide into June and at the bottom it is full summer
     right on the one-hundred-and-eighty-degree mark.
We sweat our way back through the southeast at the
     number five, and finally rise through declining numbers
to autumn, winter's chill, and the last hopeful holidays.
     At midnight of the last day of the year, I place my year in a file,
 in front of the year before, and begin again.
     I find a certain appropriateness to this system, starting a
year with big numbers, but more, for me, it reflects the
     reality of a year in a temperate climate with four seasons.
I start at the north of my flat circular year when it is cold
     and work my down to a warm summer in the south
by the first of July and then begin the return to winter.
     Anyone living at the equator or in the southern hemisphere
might not find this a useful concept. Perhaps
     they lay the circle flat or turn it upside down.
It still gets you through the year.

Beware

There can be comfort in small attainment,
an unrighteous self-forgiveness,
usurpation of judgment, the untaxed
boredom of the ordinary.

I suppose there are those who should not seek
to live beyond the quotidian,
the ever-knowable fire-warmed village,
the narrow tribe.

But beware the false modesty of the supposedly undesired,
the spoken negation of a want,
the unsought pursuit of an undeserved goal,
the unstriven.

If boundaries have always been set,
to remove them is cruel,
not the least for the tribe,
the now exposed.

To desire beyond your limits is to invite madness,
cultivates unkind comparisons
and mocks individual truth.
Is not fun.

The subconscious has its own agenda
and legitimacy lurks there,
calling out the daily lies and
disturbing comfort.

Storm

Two nights ago, there was a storm, one of late summer
with gusting winds and blowing rain and exuberant and frequent
lightning.
   It was a storm with passion and intent, rain slewing sideways,
churning and seeming to boil in the relentless lash
of the wind.
   Like most summer storms it was short lived, born of the
heat of late day, building through the late afternoon
into violence.
   The storm tested the mettle of the trees, the firmness
of their roots, the strength of their limbs and branches, and
not all survived.

   In the morning, in the park, I found a pine that had been
      pruned
by the storm, half its slender branches laid out across the grass
and on the topmost sat a quartet of Bluejays, vibrant in their
uniforms.
   They were spaced like sentries, peering off across the meadow-
like space before them, especially sharp-looking in bright blue
with shining highlights like epaulets, victoriously watching
as Flickers pecked nervously across the lawn.

Further up the hill, an old Maple lay twisted in a definition
of agony, the sheer power of the storm revealed in the obscenely torn
and splintered trunk, the anguished strips of bark, peeled like skin
and hanging in shreds.

The new wood of the outer trunk had hidden a dark and dead
heart
in the ancient tree, else the tree would have survived, but the
same weakness that inflicts a human soul had spelt death here,
and the storm had reached to its very roots.

Dance

It occurs to me that all of nature is a dancehall,
    and all things in nature, from insects to birds,
and grass to trees, to water, all dance.
    What I don't understand is why it took humans
so long to catch on, and why it took the
    Spanish and their new world children, the Africans
and their descendants, to capture
    the movements and the grace and the music.
Perhaps it was the one thing of grace
    permitted them?

Perhaps because the music of nature
    is embedded in the very flow of water,
in the wind that stirs the grass and the wheat,
    in the sloughing of pine boughs or the
sighing of branches flexing back from gusts,
    even in the dust swirling in the dirty streets,
perhaps this was the one unfettered,
    uncontrolled gift, that no master or
landlord could tax, market, or enslave?

Of course, the English developed a Waltz
    and the Viennese sped it up, but these
were dances for the gentry, the well-dressed
    and the well-fed, not the servants in
livery or the butler at the door holding cane, hat.
    It took the Cubans in the sugarcane

fields to make the shuffle of the Cha-Cha,
 to dance it to the violin of a Cuban composer,
and the poor along the Rio de la Plata,
 the African descendants in the slums
to dance the Tango, to celebrate a less
 fettered sensuality, to apply energy to
joy, and not to hard labor.

The Cubans, the mix of Spanish and Africans
 again, created the Rumba and the Mambo,
and the Samba, all born in the forest
 and rainy villages of equatorial Africa,
one of the few places where the natural
 world never permitted you to ignore it.

All of these dances from the Indies and
 the Caribbean, from the hard places of
South America down by Argentina, all
 of them carry a freedom, a natural
sensuality, a memory of a wilder, untamed
 life in a hot place, where rains pour
from the sky like the end of the world,
 where lightning crashes like cymbals
in the dark night and wind thrashes
 village and roof and forest,
threatening to tear the heart from you.

So when you are chained to a new future,
    when your body is all you have left
to call your own, and not even all of that,
    your spirit calls out for music
and a primitive, pure response, through
    fast-stepping feet, swaying hips
and the grasp of a good man or
    a good woman in your arms.

Latitudes, Platitudes

While not yet night, was stormy now, darkness soon to come,
Sunnyvale Home,

Repository of middling truths, perceived wisdom, tortured phrases,
platitudes the

Conversational lubricants on the downward slope to and through
the tunnel of senility

And good intentions poorly conceived and more poorly spoken.
Calm gone.

Not my cup of tea, says Maude, that belongs to Mel, and why did
you give me a lemon,

I'm not trying to make lemonade? Waste not, I say, waste not that
lemon lest you

Want it tomorrow, which is another day, of course. Unless, well best
not assume, you ass.

Tomorrow and tomorrow, I've been waiting for the good thing to
come, and if I get any weaker

I won't be able to hold the kitten. By the way, what's that writing on
the wall, shouldn't someone

Clean it off? I took my medicine but I'm not laughing about it. My pants are in a twist, and my

Gold has lost its glitter. I need something to shine it with. And Mel just went around the corner,

Which I guess means he'll come around tomorrow. It's just a matter of time, now that he's no longer fit as a fiddle and old as the hills, no longer brave as a lion, too rough to be a diamond,

I tried to kiss and make up but he thinks I'm ugly as sin without a care in the world

And his tail is between his legs. He woke up on the wrong side of the bed this morning and fell on his ass.

So it goes. I'll have to forgive and forget I guess, time heals everything, no need to cry over spilled milk,

The horse has left the barn, Rome wasn't built in a day, and if at first I don't succeed I'll try again and

See if I can get his sorry ass in bed. I need to just work smarter, not harder, winners never quit, I've heard, but I need to think outside the box and it will all look better in the morning.

They say you can't judge a book by its cover, and there are plenty more fish in the sea, but perception is reality and patience is a virtue, but God is giving me more than I can handle right now. I ate my cake, but I still want it, the customer is always right, and I want another piece of the pie. The more things change around here, the more they stay the same, all fair in love and war, and all men are created equal but that bastard's beauty is only skin deep. I'm gonna knock his block off, gossip is the devil's radio, and I'm going to give him a piece of my mind. It doesn't matter if you win or lose. We'll all look back and laugh at this someday. Everything works out in the end and this too shall come to pass. We're all in this together, unfortunately. What's done is done, only dead fish go with the flow. We are where we are. Love means never having to say you're sorry. I can't be sad it happened, only glad it's over. Or whatever, maybe it's the other way around. As I said, what goes around comes around and what goes up must come down, lets don't reinvent the wheel, follow your passion, follow your bliss, it's not rocket science, money can't buy happiness, and each moment we are living might be our last here. I hope God has a plan, because I sure don't. C'est la vie.

Novella

and

Short Stories

Journey

It has been more years than I care to count since I met Roberts. And we lost touch not long after we met. I did try to locate him for a specific reason which I will explain later, but I had misgivings very early on. He made me uncomfortable at several levels. For one—and I'll just get this out of the way immediately—I was a bit envious of him, or at least of his enthusiasm and energy, as I was struggling in my own career, travelling for business too much, often to sweaty third-world capitals where nothing happened on time or without a bit of cash to make it happen. And I was dealing with smarmy, over-dressed, under-educated, self-important civil servants and military creatures with long fingernails and short attention spans.

In spite of my uneasiness, we ended up spending parts of several weeks together in one of those sweaty capitals. And over those weeks, in bars and beach clubs, he told me how he had come to be there and laid out his plans. His enthusiasm worried me. It was bundled in a cloak of naïve expectations and an overly generous view of his fellow human beings.

When he talked about the project he was pursuing, it was like listening to a person talk about winning at the casino, or telling you about a scheme that would make him wealthy while knowing it's a scam. He was close to my age, and I felt he should have been wiser. He had already invested his time and other people's money in something that my experience on the continent told me was almost certain to fail for a long list of reasons.

The night before I was due to fly out to another city down the coast, we met at a newer restaurant out by the beach south of the city, where the food was mostly European in origin and nature, the wine was French, and the service was remarkably efficient for the city. I was paying for dinner knowing Roberts was on a tight budget. And I also wanted to show a bit of generosity of spirit and cash and to show myself that I really didn't resent his enthusiasm so much after all.

We finished dinner about ten and took a taxi together back to the city. The taxi dropped him off at a street corner not far from the center of town. He said his hostel was just up the hill. I went on to my own hotel, the most expensive in town, a few miles away. As I was getting out of the taxi, I noticed a notebook or small journal on the seat which must have fallen out of Roberts's pocket as he got out. We were only a short distance from where Roberts had gotten out, so I asked the driver to go back to that corner and I would see if I could find the hostel, although Roberts had not mentioned its name. We looked in vain and found nothing that resembled a hostel or rooming house. After five or ten minutes of searching I told the driver to just take me to my own hotel where I would see if the journal had anything of importance in it, and either leave it at the embassy or look for Roberts next time I was in this city.

I was tired when I got to the hotel. In the morning, I would have to deal with getting to the airport. I was hoping that the scheduled flight would be on time and actually going where it was supposed to go. Occasionally if a flight was running late, the pilot would just skip a city or two on the route in order to make it back to the home country as scheduled, which always pleased the airline management. I threw the journal in my suitcase and finished most of the packing for departure. In the morning, an article of clothing must have been covering the journal and I forgot about it until I landed later that day and unpacked.

I had appointments and meetings for three days and didn't think to look at the journal until the evening of the fourth day when a client cancelled our dinner meeting because of a family problem. I ate alone in the hotel restaurant and went back to my air-conditioned room for the night. I took the journal out and perused it. It turned out to be a sort of diary, plus snippets of stories Roberts had apparently written after some of his experiences and notes for other stories. The journal seemed to go back a number of years, and I could begin to see the source of Roberts's enthusiasm for the continent. I vowed to make an effort to return the journal to him if at all possible. He had been planning to stay in that coastal country and would no doubt check in at the embassy if he had not done so already. That was always prudent in those days. I could leave the journal there for him.

It was to be nine months before I returned to that city. I had brought the journal back with me, and had not read any more of it, since it was, after all, a private diary of sorts. On my third day back in the country I took the journal with me to the American embassy and told the receptionist what I wished to do. She was an exceptionally attractive local young woman, and she asked me to wait while she called a cultural attaché or some such official who appeared a few moments later and escorted me past security to an elevator for a lift up to the third floor. I had been in the embassy before and met with their business development people but had never met this fellow. I have forgotten his name now, but that is of no consequence.

I told him about the circumstances surrounding my having the journal and asked if he were the right person to leave it with. I told him Roberts's full name and enquired if he might have checked in with the embassy. The attaché frowned when I told him Roberts's name and asked again how I knew him. I told him about our chance meeting nine months ago.

"Well, I do know of Mr. Roberts. He was quite involved in a project here. But I'm afraid Mr. Roberts is dead."

"Good Lord, how can that be? How did he die?"

"Car crash, happens all the time, as I'm sure you know in these places."

"When did this happen? I think it's been about nine months since I met him. I expected to be back before now."

"It was about three months ago. We don't have many Americans die here. Stands to reason, there aren't many of us here to begin with."

"I know," I said.

"So, do you have information on his family, or where the body was sent in the States? I'd like to get this journal back to them. It might be meaningful."

"He's buried here. We couldn't locate any family."

"How can that be?" I asked. "He must have had contact information or addresses in his passport."

"Well, we did have contact information for a General Dunneworth, I think his name was, but he was not helpful. He claimed he didn't know the man's family. The General had some issues here, so I think he wanted to distance himself. Maybe the journal you have would help us locate someone."

I don't know what prompted me to lie at that point. I had the journal in my attaché case.

"Of course, I'll just have to pop back to the hotel and get it. I was just passing after an appointment at the ministry and thought I would check to see about leaving it."

I'm not sure the attaché believed me, but he didn't challenge me. "No problem, just drop it off when you have a chance, and we'll see if that helps us locate family. How long are you here on this trip, by the way?"

"I'm not sure," I replied. "These trips never go the way you expect. Appointments don't always mean much, as I'm sure you've encountered."

"Too true, yes. Well, just leave the journal with the receptionist with attention to me when you have time."

As I said, I don't know why I lied about not having the journal. When I think back on it, I recall thinking that before I gave it up, I'd like to know a bit more about the man whom I had both momentarily envied and feared. I don't believe in auras or such. To me, that's nonsense. But Roberts had an energy and a spirit about him that attracted your attention and drew you in. And for him to have died in such an insultingly ordinary way seemed wrong, or misplaced. I also was curious about this General the attaché had mentioned, and about the farm project Roberts had been so enthusiastic about. I hadn't thought to ask the attaché about that.

I had only one more meeting that day, and by mid-afternoon I was free. I took the journal to the patio at the hotel. It was ringed by palm trees and colorful tropical plants and had umbrella-shaded seating areas, a bubbling water fountain, and comfortable chairs grouped near a bar that served drinks and light lunches and snacks.

I ordered a Heineken and some mixed nuts and began to read.

It took me about three hours to read through the entire journal. Had it been typed and easily legible, I could have read it in an hour. But it was handwritten and not always clearly, and there were arrows and revisions and crossings out and pages out of sequence.

By the time I had sorted out the whole journal, it was close to dinner time. I decided that I would piece together the story of Roberts's life, or at least the pieces that he had revealed in this journal. It would become a kind of tribute to his too-short life. I was quite fascinated by the story he had told in sketches and jumbled paragraphs in the journal. I also felt bad that I had not tried harder to find him and get it back to him before he died. It would take me several months to put the material into a good readable format.

I should also mention that I met Roberts on a layover between flights. At that time, Pan Am was the only airline that flew to that part of Africa from the US, and several nights per week a 707 airliner would depart from the Pan Am terminal at JFK airport in New York and in the morning would land in Dakar, in Senegal, and then continue on down the coast stopping in most of the capitals of the former British colonies across the continent. But it skipped the French colonies and the smaller British ones, and if you wanted to go there you were obliged to disembark somewhere along the line and wait for an Air Nigeria DC 9 which sooner or later might show up to take you where you really wanted to go. Or you could fly to London and catch the weekly VC10 that had BOAC painted on one side and the colors of the host country painted on the other.

Most people coming from the States chose the Pan Am option and connections on the continent. Roberts and I met at the bar after disembarking from the Pan Am flight late that morning. We were the only two passengers due to fly further that day and we struck up a conversation.

I had lost count of the number of times I had been out to these countries as a sales representative for a multinational provisioning company. But this was only Roberts's third trip to the area. He had a dream of developing a business out there, and it was this dream, this vision, that had generated feelings of both the envy and the concern that I mentioned earlier.

By the time I finished reconstructing the journal and assembling a timeline, I had a more complete understanding of both why I had envied him briefly and why I had felt concern for him.

(Please note that some of what follows are Roberts's own words, taken directly from his journal. Other sections are my own edits and constructions based on his notes and disjointed writings. I believe it all captures what he felt and thought.)

Section 1

I had dreamed of Africa from an early age. But the Africa I dreamed of was the Africa of H. Rider Haggard, not the Africa of the former British and French empires, or the Africa of a realistic geography. My Africa was a continent with only a fringe of population along its coasts, a land of elephant graveyards, undiscovered mountains beyond which lay yet undiscovered plains and valleys waiting for the touch of the plow and civilization. The jungles and wild lands of my continent would have welcomed Tarzan, and he would have been comfortable there.

My Africa had no history of slave trading or of colonization, no memory of a morally bankrupt and supremely evil Belgian king, nor did it include amongst its primitive little nations a country defined by racial segregation. It was benign and mostly vacant and waiting for me to arrive and settle its forgotten heart.

A person might be forgiven, or at least given a purgatorial pardon, for holding such beliefs when you take into account the biased history of the North America frontier that was taught at the time in America's schools. In that history an enlightened vanguard of often formerly-oppressed pioneers, pure of heart and with the best intentions for all of mankind, rid slopes and prairies of a sparse population of ignoble savages and dotted these prairies with schoolhouses, tiny churches, and the word of a well-seasoned God.

Much of Africa lay in want of just such a transformation, and I still believed in God and the power of virgins back then. I could conquer at least a part of it. The very names of places beckoned. There was a Gold Coast that suggested gold for the taking. And an Ivory Coast, which spoke of endless herds of elephants, even though in reality, it was most of the width of the continent away from the elephants, the hippos, the lions and giraffes, the rhinos.

Plus, my soon-to-be good friend Tarzan was out there waiting for me. Jane, who knew.

Of course, all of those notions were products of my childhood, but they still were there in the back of my mind. And while I knew better, a part of me always wanted it to be the way I had dreamed of it at the age of six or seven. Besides, even though my knowledge of the continent had improved dramatically in the intervening two decades, there remained much to generate confusion. South Africa was a country, but North Africa was an entire region of the continent.

Lord Jim and the journals of Sir Richard Burton had disavowed me of notions of a temperate climate and any kind of seasonal normality. Kilimanjaro had snow at the peak and the Kenyan highlands were known as the land of eternal springtime. I wrote the Sahara off since I didn't plan to go there, and it didn't fit with my needs.

And I was especially unhappy with Great Britain for giving up its colonies. I remember the day that my grandfather came in with the evening paper that had been placed in a little round metal container by the driveway and announced that Britain was giving up its empire because it could not afford to keep it. It seemed like a poor excuse to me and an abandonment of all that I felt the small island had done to advance and improve the world, further evidence of the vaunted education system of the day, although admittedly, no other view would really have been taken seriously at the time.

I just didn't see how the colonies could be ready to be free. Sir Richard Burton and John Speke had had to discover the source of the Nile. How could you set free the territories and infant nations who didn't even know their own geographies and couldn't find the sources of their own rivers? Hadn't Livingston gone out there and been lost for years? No maps. How would the new nations even know where their borders were?

I wasn't, of course, as totally ignorant of the place as it sounds. I had an imperfect knowledge of Darwin's work and had mistakenly included Africa in it. And while the early peoples of East Africa—another region, not a country—would be found to be the key to human development, I did not include them in my own plan for the dark continent. In fact, I think I was mostly focused on Darwin's dimly-lit study in his house back in England. I had seen a photograph of it in a Life magazine special edition book on evolution, and I wanted such a room in the sprawling colonial headquarters I would construct in my new native land.

If I had paid full attention to Hazzard's story, had looked into the accounts of travelers other than Burton and Speke from earlier years, had examined geographies more closely, I would have understood the utter dominating ignorance of my vision. But dreams are seldom based on verifiable realities. They lodge themselves in the subconscious where they promote what they wish. The real world doesn't matter.

By the time I finally set foot on the continent for the first time, the British and French had handed their colonies over to the local people, had created countries that had no relationship to past tribal loyalties, and had decamped back to their homelands.

But for me, there was one more event that helped to prolong my dream of coming out to this continent and helping with a bit of nation building. I had given up on finding a hidden valley and building a sprawling plantation, but there was much work yet to be done. There was talk of new leadership from young, European-educated Africans who might become the new philosopher-kings of the post-colonial world. It was about that time that I found myself on a train from London to Salonica, the Simplon Orient Express, the poor cousin of the elegant Orient Express of murder mystery fame.

I had managed to stay in the first-class section of the train by offering a small token of my appreciation to the conductor to supplement my second-class ticket. This was from Trieste, and the train was packed with passengers from Yugoslavia who had gone to Italy to shop and were now heading back to Belgrade and several stops along the way before the train would split with one section going to Istanbul and the other to Athens. It was a slow train, pulled by a steam engine that burned a very smelly sulfurous coal, and the concept of air-conditioning had not yet come to rail line.

In the compartment that I had managed my way into there was a woman in her fifties who was headed back to Athens from Paris. She was a ballet teacher and had spent the summer at workshops and performances in France. Given my quite meager exposure to such levels of culture at the time, I was quite impressed that people might travel from one international capital to another for a whole summer just to pursue an occupation and to learn. The only comparison I could offer up would have been the experience of a first-grade teacher who drove fifteen miles to a teachers' college for two summers to attain a master's degree.

More fascinating than the ballet instructor, however, was a young man from Kenya, who had been studying in Europe and was headed back to the newly independent nation of Kenya to be in charge of the department of Agriculture. Or so he said. I have no idea if he was truly going to start out, at the age of no more than twenty-eight or thirty, as I assumed him to be, as one of the top government officials in this newly independent nation. It didn't matter. While he might not be the equivalent of a Thomas Jefferson or a John Adams in this new role, he was nonetheless going to have a hand in nation building. I envied him the opportunity. But more, even though it would be nearly a decade before I would have the time and resources to begin working on the continent, I would never forget that meeting on the train from Paris. It was with regret that I stepped down from the carriage at midnight in Salonica.

Section 2

As noted, it was a few years before I first was able to set foot in the country. When I look back on it, I am in some ways amazed that I survived the first trip or two. I will recount only one of the evenings, but it will tell you a bit about my level of near recklessness.

I believe that it was my second night in the country, and someone I met at the hotel bar recommended a club near the beach that had great music to dance to, lots of girls looking for some fun for the evening, and cheap drinks. I took a taxi to the club after dinner, which was over by eight o'clock. Night falls in the tropics around six in the evening the year around, and by eight or nine it has usually cooled off from the oppressive heat of the day. The beachside of the city and the expatriate villas in the hills above the beach get cooling breezes from the ocean, and the club was located several miles out beyond a long stretch of beach near a casino.

It was a great location for a dance club. Dance floor open to the sky, strings of colored lights, great sound system, well-stocked bar—more like something you would expect in Miami or southern California. I went up to the bar to order a beer, and while I was standing there a tall, slightly thin local girl came up and ordered one as well. She glanced at me as I recall, and I smiled and offered to pay for her drink. She accepted. We talked of nothing for a moment or two and then went to the dance floor. It was midweek, but the club still filled to at least half capacity as the evening wore on. The dress was casual—shorts and skirts for the women, mostly shorts and casual shirts for the men. I continued to dance with the girl, whose name was Suzy, for the entire evening, and we drank beers and occasionally took a break for her to smoke a cigarette. At one in the morning, we ended up in a taxi together.

I next recall waking up around seven the next morning, and for a few moments the switchboard in my brain seemed to have shut down. No messages were getting from the brain to the body, and none were being received. But gradually the circuits began to warm up and clear, and several very strong rectangles revealed themselves to be a door opening and a window frame. The puzzlingly inappropriate overhead parallel lines resolved into a corrugated, tinny ceiling of galvanized metal. Now that I had figured out that I was in a room, I tried next to establish the location of the room. Here I was at a loss. I only knew it wasn't in my hotel, which had a plastered concrete ceiling.

Working backward, my brain recognized a period of sleep, several sensual disturbances on which it seemed not to be able to focus. Disappointing. There were images of a jumble of streets and alleys on which this room must be located. Before I could carry this analysis any further, there was a sudden swaying jostling of the bed, and I realized there must be someone else in the bed with me. The dark-skinned girl from the night before got up from the other side of the bed naked and yawning. She made her way to a door. I heard a latch bolt slide out of its catch and hinges creak as the door to the outside was pulled open, releasing a splash of sound from a courtyard. The girl didn't close the door, and I wondered if she had just gone out into the courtyard naked or if she had pulled a piece of cloth, a lapa around her waist. I don't know why that seemed important.

Sounds continued to bubble in from outside. A baby was squalling, two women were arguing in an upcountry tribal language with staccato emphases, and someone was polishing rice with a large mortar and pestle that set the beat with its cushioned 'thock.'

In spite of the freshness of the day, I recall thinking that the morning had already been saturated and spoiled by all of this noise and activity. The day had been thrust upon me. At the same time there was a certain inevitable dreariness that hung in the milky light, and nothing could possibly restore clarity and purpose. I fished around under the bed for my glasses, and once they were perched back on my nose, I could at least see where I was, but how I had come to be here was still vague.

I stood up slowly and found my khaki shorts under the bed. I remembered to check them for spiders and scorpions and centipedes and having found none, put them on. I didn't find any underwear, so I guessed I hadn't worn any. I found my shirt and did the same inspection and having found it insect free, put in on, found my sandals, did the same inspection, and put them on and went out into the courtyard. Suzy was coming out of a washhouse and toilet across the courtyard. She had tied a lapa around her waist and grinned at me and pointed at the right door. I went in, closed the door, and relieved myself.

When I returned to the room where I had woken up, Suzy was looking in a cupboard for clothes. She turned to me and said, "I need to bathe and head to work. You can leave when you wish, but tell my Auntie so she can lock up. She's the one polishing the rice. Will you be at the club again tonight?"

Suzy was clearly better at this than I was. I was hungover and barely functional. "No," I said, "I'm afraid not, I have to go up-country today. Maybe another night."

"That would be nice," she said as she gathered up her clothes and a towel.

I was unclear on whether I owed Suzy any money for the night. I finally said, "I had fun, can I give you a little money for expenses, whatever…"

"If you wish. I don't do it for the money, but that would be nice."

My money was still in the pocket of my shorts, and I fished out the equivalent of five dollars in local currency, which was more than the daily wage of the average citizen, and she thanked me. "I hope to see you again sometime," she said and went out to the washhouse.

I found my way out of the maze of alleys to a street that had taxis passing and took one back to my hotel, where I downed three aspirin, took a shower, and checked out. I took another taxi to a small garage on the outskirts of the city, where you could rent cars for as long as you needed them. The deposit was minimal. One was highly unlikely to steal the car, and no one worried about insurance. Credit cards were just coming into use at that time. Most people carried traveler's checks, and everyone paid for everything in cash.

I think that catches me up on how this whole new adventure has started. That was my first trip out here, before I had an idea that someone would actually want to follow through and attempt to grow some food.

Section 3

I suppose I should say a little something about why I am in this country now, a little about how things have gone and what I hope to do. I think that if a person were to read only the first few pages of this journal, you might think of me as a naïve idiot. And if things don't work out, maybe that's how I will be judged. But, honestly, I'm not on a mission to convert anyone to Christianity or that sort of thing. I am really just interested in food and farming.

I grew up on a small farm and always wanted to have a bigger farm, or a huge ranch, and nothing in my life up to this point has made that a possibility in the US. But a few months ago, my then girlfriend encouraged me to go to hear a speech at a local university about international development and opportunities around the globe. She knew of my interest in Africa.

The speaker turned out to be a former military leader, a general in the army, who had established contacts in Asia and Africa, and he discussed the trends in food production in Africa particularly since the colonial structure had disappeared. He gave examples of countries that had been self-sufficient in food production under the British, especially, and which were now having to import staples such as rice because the local farmers either could not or would not, according to him, put out the effort without being managed by westerners. It was quite a racist take on things, but the statistics didn't lie.

He claimed that funding was available for entrepreneurial types who would be willing to work in parts of Africa or Southeast Asia to develop farms with modern equipment. His vision was to leapfrog the evolutionary process that had occurred on American farms. No beasts of burden—straight to tractors and mechanical tillage and harvesting. To me, it made sense.

I won't go into the details of my lengthy discussions with this gentleman, but we eventually reached a trial agreement that involved him hiring me to expand on a preliminary study and to find out more about land availability and its cost, soil samples, markets, transportation, and where to get the equipment needed for such an enterprise. The deciding factor for the General, I think, was the fact that I had had enough interest on my own to have actually visited some of these countries in the past several years. I should note that by now my former girlfriend in the States had dumped me for a professor, partly because she had not expected me to become so obsessed with actually going to Africa to work and live for a while, maybe a long while. She liked seeing things from a distance.

The General had planned to come along on this trip, but something in Asia dealing with oil had become a priority, and he headed to the west coast to catch a Pan Am connection to Indonesia and sent me off to New York to go the other way. The General had been out to these countries in the preceding year, and he had files and dossiers which he'd had his secretary or assistant compile, and these included the names of government ministers and local chiefs and other business people who might be useful in various places. He met with me and gave me the files to read and absorb, I think as a test of my ability, interest, and ultimately my commitment. I apparently passed his tests, because I am now headed up-country to the location we have chosen together as the first place to begin a rice and corn plantation.

I was met in the provincial capital this evening by local government officials and by the tribal chiefs and head men for the region we were interested in. Every chief wants me to look at a piece of land in their chiefdom, because it would bring in rent, and presumably they are interested in job creation as well. It was hard to tell as this was spoken of desultorily. As in, oh yes, that would be nice.

I spent the night in a government rest house and this morning met the first of three representatives from three different chiefdoms to look at land. We were driven in a ministry Land Rover to each of the three sites, which took most of the morning. It is now my job to have each of them surveyed and to choose a house and buildings for equipment and supplies and presumably to store the harvest. We drove through several riverside towns that have clearly seen better days. One of them was an administrative center for the British, and there are empty warehouses and garages and several buildings with ramps that lead down from the buildings to concrete docks that must have been used for shipping rice to the capital. The officials confirmed that the British had cultivated rice in all of the swamps in the area, but the local people had returned to the upland and slash and burn farming because they didn't like working in the cold water of the swamps and they feared the snakes that lived there. I asked who worked in the swamps when the British ran them and they said the local people did, but they got paid and the snakes did not seem to come as often then.

The areas we have chosen to farm are the great flood plains in the south of the country. The countries in this belt have two seasons, a dry one lasting from about October to April and a rainy one from May through

September when it rains three hundred inches most years. It may rain for a month with hardly any pause.

We will plant the corn and the rice in the sections of the plain that don't flood deeply or don't flood at all and depend on the rain. The rice can be flooded, the corn cannot.

Section 4

I've been busy and haven't had much time to write in this journal. I've had five thousand acres of land surveyed, have rented a large house to live in, hired a cook, rented two warehouses, and am looking for a barge-type boat to haul the rice to the capital. I had found a dealer who will sell us the tractors and the plows and the seeders for the corn and rice. I just need for the General to wire some money or bring over a suitcase full of cash.

I'm back in the capital for a few days. I had to go to Spain to look at some rice milling equipment, and it was faster to fly back to New York and then back here than it was to wait for a connection from Madrid. I guess I could have gone to the Canary Islands and then back, but I didn't know about that. I met a fellow at the airport while we were waiting for a connection from the Pan Am flight from New York. He's a representative for a company that distributes all types of supplies across the continent. It seems that nothing of any kind is manufactured on the continent. Not even simple things like tea kettles or pottery. Certainly no equipment and no vehicles. The trucks and cars are from Germany, England, and Japan, and a few cars are from France. The merchants are Indian, Lebanese, and Syrian. Locals only run small shops.

This representative is a nice enough guy, and we have spent a number of evenings together. He is on an expense account and is quite generous, but he's quite skeptical of the project I've embarked upon. He wishes me luck, but tells me to be careful, as he has found corruption to be a serious *concern across the continent and that success is frequently resented as opposed to being celebrated. I don't feel like that kind of response should come from the benefits we plan to bring. But I do need the General to get on the stick with some cash. Kronos has been very patient with us and did go ahead and order the tractors, but he needs to be paid. Interesting guy. For someone who was so negative in the beginning he has really come around. But I still don't trust him.*

It was at this point that Roberts left the journal in the taxi and I had no idea what had happened in the months between my meeting him and his death. But I was quite curious. I was surprised to hear how much he had accomplished up to that point—land apparently surveyed and ready for use, equipment ordered, warehouses and housing in place. He would have to have opened a bank account by now and registered a company with the government.

I had my own business to attend to for a couple of days and by then it was the weekend.

One of the businessmen I sold products to invited me to a party at his house up in the hills above the beach on Saturday night. There were at least fifty people there, including some professors from the local college, business cohorts, and other expatriates. There were no other Americans there, but El Halaby, my host, introduced me to a strikingly beautiful woman, a cousin named Cyla who had just flown in that morning from Beirut.

"I know you have an eye for the ladies," he said to me, which was not really true, "so behave with my cousin. She is very smart."

He turned to Cyla. "My friend here is not bad for an American, maybe you will find him interesting." He patted me on the shoulder and laughed and left us alone.

"What was that all about?" I asked. "It's very nice to meet you."

"No idea. He's just a jokester. You are from the company that makes the things he sells in his stores?"

"Not the company that makes them, the company that distributes them."

"Ah, an American company."

"No, a Dutch company, as it turns out."

"And how did you happen to go to work for a Dutch company? That's not very common for an American, I don't think."

"No, it's not. It was a misplaced sense of adventure. I wanted to travel, and I had learned Arabic, and the company needed someone to come out here. Now I've done it too long. What about you?"

"I'm a professor at the American University in Beirut. I teach history."

"Fascinating."

"Not really, not for the students anyway." She laughed.

"Why are you out here?" I asked.

"Family history. I'm looking into when our family and others started coming out here and opening businesses. It has been generations, hundreds of years for some families."

"I have a sense of that," I said. "I've gotten to know a lot of people over the years across this belt of Africa. It's not such an easy life, I don't think."

"It depends. It's not so bad if it's all you've known. And it's in our blood. Do you know much of the history of our country, or of the Levant?"

"A little. I know you've been parts of a lot of Empires, got taken over by the French in 1918, and that Beirut is known as the Paris of the Middle East. Does that count?"

She smiled. "That's more than most Americans know. We aren't big enough or important enough to generate much international interest, but the Levant was the trading nexus of the known world for centuries. Beirut, Baghdad, Cairo, the great cities of a century or two ago. You should come to Beirut."

I was about to respond when El Halaby returned and took me aside. "Listen, you can talk to Cyla in a bit, but I understand you knew this fellow Roberts, who was killed in a car crash recently?"

"I didn't really know him, but I have some information about him. I was sad to hear he was killed."

"Well, the cultural attaché at your embassy is an acquaintance, and I saw him on Friday, and he mentioned you and a journal?"

"Yes, but how do you know about Roberts?"

"It's a very small world out here, very, very, small. And nothing that an expat does goes unknown for more than a minute. By tomorrow you will have been rumored to have seduced my cousin and will be the object of a death threat by her brothers back in Lebanon." He laughed. "No seriously, everyone knew that he was working with some General who didn't have the money he said he had and the Greek got embroiled in the project. It was not pretty, but the Greek can afford it. You should talk to him."

"Is this someone named Kronos? There was an entry in Roberts's journal, his diary."

"Yeah, that's him. I surprised you don't know Kronos. He's tight with the government, has the contract for equipment, tractors for their stupid plowing scheme. Has a wife back in Athens and mistresses here and probably every other city he does business in. His family has a trucking company in Syria I think it is. Lots of money. Very charming guy by the way. Unless you piss him off. But not as bad as the Turks, who he hates. So do I, by the way, but that's for another day.

"Anyway, look him up on Monday, he's just down from the Embassy. Now you can go back to talking to Cyla."

Meanwhile Cyla had been taken over by a group of professors from the local college, and every time she made an effort to step away, another teacher of some sort was introduced and I gave up. After talking to a few of the people I knew from business dealings, I left.

On Monday, I did as Al Halaby had suggested and found Kronos at his business, which was named InterCommerce International, which seemed to cover all the bases. He was sitting in an office that had a window that looked onto a showroom filled with pumps and generators and a wide array of mechanics tools and what looked like specialty equipment for the construction industry. He came out to greet me when I stepped in, and when I told him what I was interested in, he invited me back to his office and told an assistant to bring us coffee.

"I don't think we've met, have we?" he said, after the coffee was delivered.

"No. I'm surprised in a way, but I don't deal in the types of things you sell."

"Well, never mind. So you knew Roberts?"

"Not well. We only met over a two-week period, but I've learned a lot more since then. He left a journal, a kind of diary, in a taxi one evening, and I was attempting to return it when I learned of his death."

"So how far did this journal go? Did he talk about the farm project up-country?"

"The journal ended about the time he had just rented all the land and warehouses and ordered equipment through you it seems. That's when he left the diary in the taxi by accident."

"I see, so what do you want? Why are you interested? You're not family, right?" I could sense more than a little hostility.

"No, it was just a chance meeting. But, he had an intriguing backstory and seemed very confident and hopeful that this farming thing could work."

Kronos sat quietly and looked at me for a few moments. He was a handsome man, trim, fit, and tanned, with slightly curly hair, strong chin, and clear black eyes. He looked like he worked out and was dressed in expensive slacks and a fitted golf shirt. I had noticed that he was wearing expensive Italian shoes when he came out to greet me. There was a gold watch on his wrist, probably a Patek Phillipe.

"Yes, it was quite an intriguing story. I still can't believe I did what I did. I'm not sure I want to go over it again. It's done, he's dead, unfortunately, and there is no farm, no rice, no corn, nothing but some used equipment. Disaster."

"I wondered."

"Oh? Based on what? Are you an agriculturist? I think not."

"No, I was intrigued by his enthusiasm and by the need now that the British are gone, but I've worked out here for a long time, and he was too innocent. He didn't understand the corruption or the basics of how these people work."

"He didn't understand a lot more than that. Listen, I don't have time for this right now. Meet me for lunch at The National at one, and I'll tell you as much as I want to, enough to give you the big picture anyway. Then you leave me alone so I'm not reminded of how stupid a person can get."

With that he picked up a black phone receiver on his desk and shooed me out of the office.

I was staying at The National, so having lunch there was simple. Kronos showed up a few minutes late and was greeted by name by the hostess.

"Put us in the corner, somewhere private," said Kronos.

When we were seated, he asked for a gin and tonic, and I stayed with sparkling water. The lunch special was a Jollof rice, which we both ordered.

"Where did you say this journal left off?" he asked.

"He had just finished the land surveys for a few thousand acres and rented warehouses and somewhere to live. And I think had ordered equipment from you. He mentioned that you were waiting for payment from the General."

"Ah, the useless General. Or worse. Okay, I'll give you the—how do you say?—'quick and dirty' version of what happened. This General did finally pay a deposit, about a hundred thousand US dollars. He supposedly was waiting for some money for or from an oil concession in Indonesia. I don't know, he probably made it up. He was full of shit.

"But, at any rate, I had ordered the equipment, some tractors, plows, disks, tillers and corn planter and seed drill for the rice. I had orders in for tractors for the government, so it was best to do it all together to have a combined shipment. A lot of it comes from South Africa.

"And this was my first mistake. I would never agree to anything without payment first. It is my only rule, but I had convinced myself that Roberts actually had a good idea and that his could work.

"He had soil tests, and he had an expense and revenue summary that looked realistic based on the market prices of corn and rice. Both are imported here at high cost, as you must know. And the demand will only go up, and the cost of imports will only go up. And this General did wire a hundred thousand, so that's still a lot of money. Did Roberts mention what this whole project was supposed to cost?"

"No, there were no numbers of any kind in the journal. It was more personal."

"Well, I guess he had another journal for that. Anyway, this was to cost almost a million by the time we got in the harvesters and the seeds and trained and paid laborers, and fuel, which is a fortune here as you know, and then the processing and bagging equipment. There's no infrastructure of any kind here, in spite of the British having been here for so long. It was either small scale or it has been stolen or fallen into disrepair.

"At any rate, we get the equipment, the General is still not sending money, so I pay for the tractors and the seeds and we have everything we need to start so I go ahead and advance money for the fuel and the laborers, and Roberts hires some managers, who lie to him all the time about why they aren't getting the work done, and some fuel gets stolen, and at one point some local farmers whose land got given away by the chief, damage a couple of tractors, and this is where I should have taken over and hired some security I could trust, but I didn't. Maybe it wouldn't have mattered because we needed fertilizer for the corn, did I mention fertilizer? No, I don't think so. So the local agriculture department had some warehouses full of bags of fertilizer that were supposed to be used on oil palms, but the government ministers had used all the money for the project to pay themselves for land that wouldn't work for oil palms, had cleared it and now had no money to actually plant the trees. They agreed to sell the fertilizer to Roberts at a discount. But the problem was the fertilizer had sat around in damp warehouses for three or four years and was in hard blocks and much of the value had leached out or whatever. And it had to be re-crushed by hand to even get it to go through the planters."

"But you did eventually plant something?"

"Yeah, yeah, he eventually planted about a hundred and fifty hectares of corn and two hundred and fifty hectares, maybe more, of rice."

"Well, that was a good start."

"Ha, yes, I guess you could say so. At least it limited the size of the disaster. You don't have monkeys in America, do you? Of course not. And you have weed killers you put on your fields, so the corn grows but not the weeds. Roberts didn't think we would need that. They could cultivate the corn or something or weed it by hand. I don't know, it didn't work."

"Didn't Roberts work with any agronomists or local agricultural people on this?"

"Yeah, he had some people from the agriculture college, but they'd been trained by the Brits and were too academic and research-oriented to be practical, if you ask me. I met one or two and thought they were useless or worse."

"Well, did you harvest anything? Surely it wasn't a complete failure."

"It was close to that. I forgot to mention that the rains came late and he had to replant the corn, which the weeds got, and what corn did make ears in some of the wetter places, the monkeys ate. There was a holdup on getting a combine harvester for the rice, which was a blessing in disguise for me, but we had to harvest the rice by hand, and half of it got stolen."

"And the General never came through with any more funds?"

"Not a cent. I don't think he ever had it. Roberts was a fool. I was a fool."

"What was going on with him during all this time? Was he overseeing it all?"

"As well as he could. I actually felt bad for him. When I wasn't furious with him and at myself, that is. But it was all very disappointing and depressing. You know, you've worked out here. This is nothing whatsoever like doing business in your country where you have laws and legal agreements and courts that work. Out here you depend on family and bribes and connections, and you make sure you have the power to control. You don't trust anyone outside your family. Even then you have to be careful sometimes. That's just how it works. That's where I was stupid. I should have realized Roberts had none of those things. He just had a vision."

"Did he kill himself? Was he that depressed?"

"No, not really, although in a sense he did. You never drive anywhere at night except in the capital or bigger towns in this country. And even that is risky, because these people have no sense when it comes to cars and trucks. They will leave broken-down vehicles in the road with no reflectors or lights or no warning devices of any kind. And by the time you see the lorry, you are about to hit it. Let me tell you a story. There was a big party about a hundred and fifty kilometers out of town a couple of months ago, and at midnight, a carload of people head back here, and after maybe thirty kilometers, whatever, there's a lorry full of palm kernels broken down in the road. The car hits it at high speed, kills everyone in the car. The lorry driver takes off into the bush, some locals get the bodies out of the car, and an hour later, another carload of people hit the same lorry and kill everyone in that car."

"Holy crap!"

"Roberts was driving back to town, different night, different road, but the same thing happened. He hit a parked lorry, and the crash killed him. I had told him never to drive at night out here."

"That's a terrible story all around."

We had been served our lunch and picked at it while we talked. I had lost much of my appetite thinking about what had happened with Roberts. I felt a bit ashamed and guilty that I had envied him when I met him.

"I know you need to get back to your office," I said to Kronos, "but could such a scheme or project ever work out here? I mean, I know there's uncultivated land all over the continent, and the food shortage gets worse every year."

"The only way any project like that will succeed is if a foreign company comes in and manages and controls it from top to bottom. There is too much cultural history for it to be otherwise. And that assumes you can pay enough to the government officials to keep them out of your hair. Or give them enough of it so they actually let you run your business the way it needs to be run."

I smiled when he said that. "I suppose that's what you have to do in your business."

He smiled back. "Enjoy the rest of your trip here. I'll pay for lunch."

I didn't have any appointments for the rest of the afternoon, so I decided to take a book and go out to the beach and sit and watch the waves and think about Roberts and dreams and reality.

There is a remarkable phenomenon in the African countries that border the Atlantic that have the narrowly defined dry seasons and rainy seasons. Particularly at the end of the rainy season, at sunset, the clouds will be colored in brilliant reds and oranges and yellows from horizon to horizon. The sunset brilliance is not confined to the western edge of the sky. This is because there are no clouds over the ocean and as the sun dips to the night horizon its light can penetrate beneath the clouds if the land is flat, and no mountains interrupt the sun's last rays of the day.

I don't see this very often because my business doesn't take me up-country, and the effect is muted here in the capital. But on the occasions when I have seen it, it feels like a blessing, one good thing over a troubled land.

Roberts would have seen those sunsets on a daily basis as his harvest was failing and his dream of building something new for Africa was coming to an end. I wonder if he saw those glittering drops of water as a mockery, and turned his back and went into his old colonial house and shut the door.

George's Mother's Chicken

George's mother, Edna Benson, had made the best fried chicken in the county. George's favorite meal, for as long as he could remember, had been fried chicken, mashed potatoes and gravy, and homemade biscuits. In a single sitting George had been known to eat three breast portions, four legs and thighs, and a half dozen gizzards.

But when George, at the age of twenty-nine, married Betsy, who was twenty-six herself, the fried chicken dinners, of which there had been at least two a week, not counting Sunday, came to an end. Betsy could eat a little chicken, say half a drumstick or a slice of nice white meat from the breast, but she could not stand to cook it.

She claimed that the feel of chicken flesh, uncooked, made her ill. Even looking at it made her nervous. And George, who had never cooked a meal in his life, was not likely to take up cooking at the age of twenty-nine, not even frying his beloved chicken.

Instead they ate pork, and sometimes beef when they could afford it, and occasionally catfish from the catfish farm down by Porterville, but never from the river since the river was polluted and ran varying colors of blue and black and red from the fabric mill upstream. It stank on warm summer nights.

Only once a month did they eat chicken, and that was when they went home to Mother Benson's after church on the first Sunday. It was the highlight of George's week; he looked forward to it for days to come and remembered it for days afterward. Having taken twenty-nine years to find a wife, however, he did not let on that the meal meant so much to him.

George had worked at the feed store since he graduated from high school. His desires, with the exception of the fried chicken, were unremarkable, and his habits were frugal. Indeed, by the time he married Betsy, he already had a house paid for, a nice bungalow that he had bought from the banker's widow and which, until he and Betsy moved in, brought in a nice little rental income. His salary was sufficient to support their not-so-great needs, and a savings account, begun during high school from part-time jobs, continued to grow.

There were those, George's mother among them, who said that what happened to George would never have occurred if only Betsy had not been so silly in her aversion to chicken. There were others who said it probably wouldn't have made any difference, seeing the way the fit caught him.

What happened was this: The Chicken King drive-in chain opened a branch in George's town, right in the lot next to George and Betsy's house. This was in the third year of George's marriage. The building was quite attractive with its neat brick sides and bright red roof. Neon lights were mounted under the eaves around the perimeter of the building giving the roof a light, airy effect, almost like floating, which George liked. A large sign was mounted in front, featuring a tall golden chicken with a crown that flashed on and off at night.

Neat "in" and "out" arrows were painted at the entrance to the paved lot around the building, and trash cans with automatic tops and plastic liners were posted at the four corners. Most neatly organized project George had ever seen.

It took two months to complete, and every evening after work George sat in his rocking chair on the front porch and admired the work going on next door, for only a low hedge separated the two lots.

When opening day arrived, the manager, a perky young man from New Jersey, came over to George's house and gave him a gift certificate for two full chicken dinners. Each included three pieces of chicken with a crunchy coating, mashed potatoes with gravy, whole wheat rolls, coleslaw, and a Dr Pepper. Betsy, who had taken a dim view of the construction project and the imminent closeness of so much chicken, nevertheless went with George in the evening for the free meal. George finished off his own meal, all of Betsy's chicken, plus a $2.39 special with only white meat, crunchy coating, and a second Dr Pepper. It was the happiest George had been in months.

The next day George told Betsy to never mind about his lunch, he'd just get some nabs or cheese. "Or chicken," said Betsy, miffed. "Who knows?" said George, but she was right.

At lunch he drove up and bought two lunch specials, and before dinner he slipped by for a ninety-nine-cent special with two pieces of chicken, no wings. To please Betsy, he ate the spareribs and homemade sauerkraut which she had fixed, but his heart wasn't in the meal.

The next day was the same. And the next. By the end of the second week, George was taking a break at ten in the morning to rush up to the restaurant for a box of legs and breasts, was back at lunch for two specials and a large order of mashed potatoes—extra gravy—and ate a bucket of wings and gizzards before supper. Betsy would still cook supper and George would still eat it, but she took to saying each morning, "Try not to eat chicken today," and in the evening, "You eat so much chicken you're going to turn into one."

Things got worse. By the end of the month, George was eating, in addition to his earlier ration, an extra two boxes of breasts, rolls, corn on the cob, potatoes and gravy, and coleslaw for supper. Betsy would cook a little something for herself and eat alone while George rocked and ate on the front porch, even though it was now late September and the evenings were cool.

In October, Betsy's sister, who was in college, came for the weekend and declared that George was suffering from a fetish brought on by lefetamines (she pronounced the "i" long, as in "copper mines"), put in chicken feed to make the chickens eat faster and get to market sooner. The lefetamines stayed in the chicken, she said, and were affecting George. George listened patiently to her explanation and then went off to buy a weekly special which featured real honey on the rolls. The conversation had made him hungry, so he had two.

In November, Betsy moved into the spare bedroom, complaining that George's skin was beginning to feel like chicken skin, damply greasy, and that the air reeked of honey, gravy grease, vinegar, and chicken.

George missed her for several nights but then adjusted. Before falling asleep he could now munch on breaded chicken livers or occasionally necks, which were sweet to suck on.

By this time George had begun to withdraw money from his savings account, much to the banker's concern, but since it was George's money there was little he could do. George still went to work properly and indeed, Mr. Mason, the owner of the feed store, said that his work had never been better.

In December, Betsy went back to her mother, "until that fool gets some sense in his head, taking second place to a chicken stand, he doesn't know I'm around," and other comments which had begun to ring of bitterness.

George scarcely noticed her absence, or if he did, he didn't mention it. But just before Christmas, George began to notice small changes in his appearance. Actually he didn't notice them so much as feel them. In the morning when he got to work he would say to Mr. Mason, "You know, I feel short today." And Mr. Mason would say, "Well George, you are short, you know, you're only five-eight. It's all that chicken you eat settling in your legs." And George would say, "That must be it," and go on with his work.

On Christmas Day the chicken stand was closed, but George bought three buckets on Christmas Eve to keep in reserve and had a lovely chicken dinner at his mother's house for Christmas. No one mentioned Betsy, who had gone to Roanoke with her mother to celebrate Christmas with her older brother.

Besides George and his mother, there were George's two older brothers, Sam and Ervin, and their wives and five children apiece. That made sixteen people, and it was later said that on what was soon realized to have been the last normal family gathering, seven large frying hens were consumed. The mashed potatoes were creamy, the gravy was smooth, the biscuits were hot, and there was plenty of honey. It was a fitting holiday feast.

It was in January that things took a more serious turn for George. He noticed several things at once. He found that he could no longer reach his flashlight and thermos jar which he kept on a high shelf in the kitchen. His pants began to drag the ground, and he had to roll them up and have the cuffs sewn by Mrs. Hawkins who lived two doors down.

His toenails became harder to cut while his fingernails grew softer. He could no longer cut through feed bag strings with his thumbnail because it would bend. Instead he had to use his knife. At the same time his hands and arms seemed to feel weaker and he was less coordinated. But his appetite for chicken went unabated. He had used up nearly a third of his savings on chicken, but now that Betsy was gone, his drain on the account was not as intense. She never asked for money.

In February, the changes became more noticeable. George had to have his pant cuffs sewn again. His shoes became too tight, necessitating a full size wider and two sizes longer. His hair began to fall out. His face was smoother and he shaved only twice a week. He wasn't certain, but he thought his nose was harder.

His eyes didn't focus as well; the edges of his glasses frames seemed to be more and more in the way. He became interested in bright sparkling objects, bits of glass, flashy stones, even the artificial rocks in the goldfish bowl. His arms seemed shorter and even less coordinated, but he still consumed copious amounts of fried chicken.

Another change had taken place as well, this one mental.

George discovered that he worried less. Even his changes were of less and less concern to him. He observed them with amusement and a certain sense of displacement, like an outsider. Simultaneously, he began to forget names and some of the details from his past. But very little bothered him. He still did his job well at the feed store.

Toward the end of February, George began to get small hard bumps under his skin from the waist up. In March, his legs became thinner and took on a distinctively yellow cast. He increased his shoe size again, his fingers seemed to be getting shorter, and his cheeks were drooping and getting pinker. His hair continued to fall out, and the bumps appeared on his head. He dressed in long-sleeved shirts and wore a hat at all times to cover the bumps, but by now his nose was definitely longer, thinner, and harder, and people began to stare. Now in addition to forgetting names, he forgot dates and days of the week. He went to work on Sunday three weeks running, not remembering that he had the day off. And for the first time, Mr. Mason had to speak to him about his work. Not that it mattered to George.

His large shoes were difficult to move around in. He had trouble remembering customers' orders, and he found that lifting bags was very cumbersome and tiring. He felt most comfortable when his arms hung loosely at his sides. He slept best in a chair or even leaning against a wall. He liked the smell of the feed at the store and continued to eat his huge daily rations of chicken from the Chicken King drive-in.

By June he could no longer use the bag cart, his hands having nearly disappeared, so Mr. Mason had to let him go. George was not concerned.

But then an even stranger thing happened. His voice began to change. In the middle of a sentence, he would suddenly emit a cluck or a cheep. To a listener this was most disconcerting, especially when George would laugh, because then his voice would disappear almost completely, and a strange cackling sound would result. George was embarrassed at first but then as the clucks grew more frequent the embarrassment subsided.

In the middle of June, George moved back to his mother's. By now he slept upright on the arm of the couch, his head tucked to one side. He had acquired a taste for sharp stones and ground feed though he still ate fried chicken. His cheeks were low and red, his nose was nearly a perfect beak, and he was nicely feathered. At his mother's he slept on the back porch perched on a low saw horse. The banister would not hold his one hundred and fifty pounds. He went to bed early and arose early.

He developed a very substantial crow that could be heard for miles and which, for his mother, was the most disturbing part of his behavior. During the day he sauntered down to the barn to look for worms or grain or to drink from the stream which ran in the near meadow. He would scratch holes with his by-now large strong claws and wallow in the smooth cool dust. When he would pick up the odd flea he would tell his mother, who would find it for him and pluck it off. Some days he would ride into town and spend a few hours at the feed store, mostly walking around among the feed sacks, savoring the aromas of soybean meal, ground corn, fish meal, barley, pelleted alfalfa, and cottonseed, or looking at back issues of *Poultry Digest.*

People were always glad to see him, and even though his ability to speak was severely limited these days, he nevertheless could get through a simple conversation.

That summer was a bad one for farmers because from the middle of May until the middle of September only one and a half inches of rain fell. The meadow stream behind the barn nearly dried up, the well ceased to produce, and Mrs. Benson had to buy water. None of this bothered George, who had found a cool glade at the upper end of the meadow, near the spring which still put out a cold narrow flow of water which collected in a round pool above some rocks and attracted insects which George found tasty. In fact, until September, life had never been so simple for George. He ate, slept, and wandered around the farm.

He still had the ability to think, but with reduced responsibilities he felt less of a need to exercise his brain. The intelligence which he possessed he preferred to keep in reserve, like money in the bank, so to speak, should the need to use it ever arise. His position gave him a feeling of great security. He never thought of himself as an animal, though other animals were curious about him. Cattle would come close to sniff him, hogs would eye him curiously, other fowl would hang back suspiciously, and dogs would bark at him but would never come close.

In September, two things occurred which came to cause George the greatest of concern. The first was this: on the fifteenth, a Sunday, it rained. Mrs. Benson was at church when the rain began, but she had left the back door ajar since the sky had been threatening when she had left at nine-thirty. She knew George would need a safe dry place to keep out of the rain.

When the rain began George was in the backyard looking for earthworms which he had recently come to enjoy but had had little luck in finding due to the dry weather. When the first drops fell, George ran to the back porch, but even there the rain was blown in by a strong south wind that had come up.

Then George noticed that the back door was ajar. He stuck his head in, pushed it open, went in, then backed up against it to close it.

It had been months since he was last in the house. It was cool and dark there, and the rain drummed smoothly on the old tin roof. George shook himself and waddled unsteadily through the kitchen to the hallway that led to the front of the house.

Memories of the days before his metamorphosis came flooding back in the sights and smells of the house, distant memories that sought to catch hold in his tiny brain but could not. Memories of a human life that was now so foreign to him seemed a reincarnation away.

At the end of the hallway was a mirror. George had forgotten about mirrors, except for the pieces of one he had consumed for his craw three weeks before. He strode up to the mirror and looked at himself, one eye at a time of course, since one was on each side of his head now. Quite impressive. His feathers were white and sleek. His legs were strong and straight with spurs beginning to appear near his old ankles. His neck was long and clean-looking, his wattles red and bright. He stretched his wings and saw that they were quite large, well fleshed, and solidly feathered right down to the tip. His beak had an elegant Roman curve to it, and his eyes were clear and alert. His head was smooth with tight small feathers, and his comb—my God, his comb! He had no comb! He lowered his head. No, it wasn't set too far back. It didn't exist.

George jumped back from the mirror, knocking over a hall tree as he did so. What a ridiculous looking chicken he must be. It had never occurred to him that he didn't have a comb. All chickens have combs. The idea so bothered him that he ran down the hall, out of the house, through the rain, and into the barn, where he sulked behind a straw pile for two days.

Finally, having alarmed his mother and the neighbors by his behavior, he came out but would not explain his absence. He became much more introspective and showed up only to eat.

Mrs. Benson spoke of his behavior to Mr. Mason, who sold her the feed for George. Mr. Mason was concerned. On the following Sunday he drove out to speak to George, for he still remembered his long responsible days at the store. Mr. Mason brought with him a book called *The Great Birds of North America*, thinking it would cheer George up. Instead it became the second major blow to George's self-esteem. George realized that as a chicken he was nothing beside the magnificent hawks and eagles in the book. He was not as graceful as the swans or ducks or geese, he couldn't even fly like crows or buzzards. He was now the lowest of the low—an ungainly old chicken, fit only for consumption. He hadn't even a comb to make him attractive.

The depression which he felt brought on a severe case of molt. His feathers fell out in bunches, leaving ugly bare spots on his back and chest. His wings became sore and he no longer felt like cleaning himself. Dirt collected on his remaining feathers. He lost his appetite. His wattles shrank and lost their bright luster, his eyes became rheumy, cracks appeared in his claws. George wanted to die. Not even his stored intelligence could snap him out of his depression.

At last a veterinarian was called, all the doctors having refused to come. John Rushmeyer, who had just finished school, appeared on a Monday morning. "I understand you've been depressed lately," said Dr. Rushmeyer. George raised one wing to his head. "In your head?"

George rubbed the top of it.

"Let me see." The vet examined it. "There's nothing there."

"I—cluck—know," said George.

"I see. You're concerned about your lack of a comb, are you? George nodded his head. "Is that all?"

George shook his head. He led the vet over to the corner of the barn where he had been sleeping lately and showed him the bird book.

"Those are all beautiful birds," said the vet.

"I know," said George sadly.

"Oh, now I understand." The vet studied George for a few minutes. "George, you're going to be alright. Give me that book."

George handed him the book, and the vet left, stopping at the house for a few minutes before returning to town. Two days later Edna came to the barn quite early and called to George who was moping in a corner. "Come to the house, son. It's important."

Inside, Mrs. Benson led him to the hall mirror and handed him a package. In it was a bright red knitted comb, tall, woolen, magnificent with eight spikes and a rakish lefthand droop. She tied it on, and George looked at it. He turned to each side and surveyed it, then turned slowly to his mother and cooed gently in her ear.

"There's more," she said. She led him to the kitchen, and there on the table was a new book. George pulled out the special glasses his mother had had made for him and surveyed the title, *Gray's Guide to Domestic Fowl.* George leafed through the first few pages. Rhode Island Reds, Rock Cornish, Speckled Cornish, Broody Walloons, Grey-Wattled Primers, and Black Princes swept before his eyes. How elegant they looked. There were Oriental Bantams with four-foot tails, brown Caucasians with sleepy combs that hid one eye, and Brahmas with their feathered feet.

After a few minutes George began to feel both shame and joy. He was ashamed of his foolish depression and of his lack of self-respect, and elated to discover that he was a member of a rather elegant group of birds after all. He thanked his mother and went off to the stream to clean himself.

By Christmas, his feathers had grown back, and he had acquired a whole collection of combs. The Rotary Club invited him to substitute for its Santa Claus who was ill, and he played the part so well and drew so much business to the tiny shopping district that the city stretched its rules and voted him Man of the Year at the January banquet.

Curiosity in this age of television is a curious thing itself. Animals and monsters plot and organize; they form kingdoms and fight wars and learn about morality and deception. They fly planes and ride motorcycles and do magic tricks every day.

It is not surprising then that after the initial intense interest in George, apathy should set in. Mr. Mason, seeing George in good spirits, was less concerned about him and asked him not to hang around the store so often. It was bad for business, he said. After a family with small children was frightened by him at the Chicken King drive-in, the perky young man from New Jersey asked George to send in for his chicken, which he still occasionally ate, especially breasts which he could hold down with his claws and pull the meat from with some efficiency. "Okey dokey,'" said George, who returned home to do what he could to help Edna, his mother, who had been ill lately.

Then in June, Edna went to bed one night with her window open and a light fresh breeze blowing in, curtains puffing like white mists by the bed and a pale blue slice of moon just coming over the barn roof. But during the night, out of the clear sky a mass of icy air slipped down from Ohio and Pennsylvania, and by morning it was nearly thirty degrees in the room. Edna, who had slept soundly, awoke with a terrible cold that became pneumonia. Two days later, she died. George's brothers, who had by now come to resent his popularity and his lack of need to work, weren't sure that he should attend the funeral, fearing that he would detract from its solemnity. Besides, there was no room in any of the cars for a one-hundred-and-fifty-pound chicken.

Poor George was heartbroken. The church was more than two miles away, but ignoring his brothers' concerns, he set out on foot. He took nearly four hours to walk the distance, and when he arrived the grave-diggers were packing in the last of the earth over the coffin. From beyond the fence, he watched them shovel on the last of the dirt and place the many lovely wreaths of flowers over the bare earth.

George realized then that he had brought nothing, but glancing down he discovered some wildflowers that had escaped the untimely frost the week before. George carefully plucked six of them, one of each kind, and when the diggers had left, he went to the grave and laid the small bouquet at the head.

He was awfully tired and awfully sad, but chickens don't cry, so George just stood quietly by the grave until dark and then fell asleep by the lovely flowers. In the morning, he returned home, sad and bitter. He walked once through the house, then through the barn and took one last drink from his cool favorite stream in the near meadow. Then he left on foot. On his back he carried his book of Domestic Fowl and his little bag of combs.

That was the last anyone in those parts ever saw of George. There are some who say he went off to the woods and died of grief, others who say he was shot by hunters mistakenly, and others who say they heard he was in the zoo up in Washington, taken there by a kindly old man who picked him up hitchhiking north of Porterville.

Theme on A New Tune

After five nights amongst my records, Newton Abbot, the music master at Trinity Presbyterian Church, knew that he had missed half a lifetime of pleasure. Trained by his mother, an organist for forty years, he knew Bach, Handel, Beethoven, and some of Haydn and Mozart, as they pertained to religious music. He knew what Martin Luther had influenced. He had never heard of Carl Orff.

Newton Abbot was forty-three. He had delicate hands with long pianist's fingers and a pale wrinkled face with warm moist seventy-year-old eyes that showed just a thin line or red at the edge of turned-out lids. He was fragile without being feminine, ascetic and monkish but not pitiable and therefore not disgusting.

In appreciation for the time with my records, Newton invited to me to a private recital of his favorite music which he played on the organ and the piano at the church. He concluded the program with "Jesu, Joy of Man's Desiring" and "Sheep May Safely Graze" by Bach. His competence made me the more incredulous at his narrow exposure to classical music.

"I am in debt to you for a lovely performance," I said afterward.

"And I am in debt to you for a wonderful broadening," he said. "This world of music which I see, it has stirred something in me, such a magic thing, I can hardly say what I feel. There is a little idea coming to me, but I won't talk of it yet. It needs some time."

A week later he came to see me.

"I have reached the height of my confidence. I will never get any better. I am too old. Now of course I can listen and advise. There is such inspiration in that music. It is sad, don't you think, that such exposure must come so late, for many—never? We are trapped in the sanctuary with a few familiar hymns. Faded flowers.

Nothing but faded flowers. Well, I'll tell you, if I do nothing else, I intend to change that. I can manage the Haydn variations. I have just come from practicing those. And of course there are no arrangements for much of what I heard. Marches are not so poorly scored for piano, I think, but so much is lost, like soldiers in bare feet. I feel it just isn't proper. So I wonder, would you be so kind as to lend me an album or two? I will treat them with the greatest of kindness and respect."

"Of course," I agreed. He chose the Pachelbel and the Respighi suite by the Academy of St. Martin's-in-the-Fields.

The following week he was back and returned the two selections. He borrowed next the album with the Albani. Then some Haydn, followed by the Rameau, some Ralph Vaughn Williams, what Flanagan I had, and several works by various people dedicated to or modeled upon Couperin.

Eventually he worked his way through at least seventy-five percent of my library, which is quite substantial. It began with Johann Pachelbel's "Canon." Then came the second "Suite of Airs and Dances" by Ottorino Respighi, followed by "Dance Suite After Couperin" by Richard Strauss, and Mateo Albani's "Sonata in D." "A Concert Ode" by William Flanagan, a "Scarlatti Sonata in B Minor," "Five Airs and Dances" by John Phillipe Rameau, four anonymous Prussian marches, "Symphony on A Hymn Tune," part of the "Water Music," a Goldberg variation, "Carmina Burana," and finally a "Concerto Grosso" by Ralph Vaughn Williams completed it.

It took over a year, and always he was profuse in his appreciation. I assumed he took the records home to listen to them.

Somewhat more than eighteen months after the lovely melodies of Pachelbel's "Canon" had first fallen on Newton Abbot's ears, he disappeared. He usually came on Thursday nights.

I had grown used to and actually looked forward to his weekly visits. It was rewarding and exciting to see the joy which he was experiencing, and to discuss the music which we had just heard. He was perceptive. For a man whose existence had been steeped in religious music, he showed a remarkable ability to understand the secular demands of Carl Orff. He spent several days trying to determine the truth about the premiere of the "Water Music." His rural beginnings made him feel particularly close to Beethoven's "Pastoral Symphony."

When he failed to appear on the Thursday night, I was disappointed but not disturbed. I called his house, but no one answered. The third Thursday was the same. By now I was truly upset. He had always been punctual and considerate, phoning if he was to be even five minutes later than usual.

I went to his house but found it dark and locked. Not knowing any of his friends I didn't know where to search for him. It also occurred to me that there was probably nothing wrong and that my concern was unfounded.

On the following Monday evening a short-haired man in double-knit slacks and a bright sport shirt came to my house.

"Is Newton Abbot here?" he asked when I opened the door. I stared at him.

"I said, is Newton Abbot here? He's your friend, ain't he?"

"My friends are my own business, and I find your approach offensive."

"Listen, you tell Newton to come down to the church and turn off that long-hair music. We ain't used the church for three weeks now. We been at the school."

"Newton Abbot isn't here, and I don't know anything about your music."

"Well by God, I'll tell you." In spite of his rudeness, I was curious to hear his story. He was chairman of the deacons, it turned out, and this is what he told me:

It had started over a year and a half ago. In each service there was a section for Organ Meditation, five minutes in which the organist usually played a quiet hymn. One Sunday, Newton had played a longer-than-usual selection, almost ten minutes. The next two weeks were the same. The fourth week he played for nearly fifteen minutes, and the minister, Reverend Clippenberger, had to cut short the sermon.

After the service Reverend Clippenberger spoke to Newton. "I think you need to cut the music back to five minutes, Newton. You're cutting into my sermon."

"Oh, but no one listens to sermons anyway, Reverend. I think you should make it even shorter. There's more inspiration in the music than in the words."

The Reverend Clippenberger, unprepared for such a response, had no reply. But the following week, Newton played for only seven and a half minutes.

For two months there were no problems. Then one Sunday instead of playing the organ during the meditation, Newton played a series of Prussian marches over the amplifying system.

"I don't understand," said Reverend Clippenberger.

"You will," said Newton.

The next week Newton went to the pastor's study and proposed that Organ Meditation be lengthened to half an hour and the sermon shortened to fifteen minutes.

"Outrageous!" said Clippenberger.

The following week the music committee, which had not met for fifteen years, called a meeting at Reverend Clippenberger's behest and announced that it would select the music to be played. Newton said fine and went ahead with a "Hornpipe" by Handel as interpreted by Ramond Leppard and the English Chamber Orchestra. It was such a moving and lovely piece of music that no one could really object, and it was quite short.

For the next few months there was a running battle between Newton and the committee. Some weeks he was obedient, others he would play his own selections on either the organ or the amplifier. When he was criticized, he merely smiled benignly and moved on.

The truth of the matter was that Reverend Clippenberger, who insisted on basing his sermons on close Biblical study, and very little on average daily behavior, was boring. Therefore, many of the parishioners, who came only out of tradition and not to gain insight, were happy to get the hour over with as painlessly as possible. The music was the lesser boring of the two possibilities. And the hint of scandal which surrounded the affair actually increased church attendance.

The breaking point came at the end of the first year, when Newton played a half hour selection from Beethoven's "Ninth Symphony." Reverend Clippenberger was furious and warned Newton never to do that again. "I will force you to stop playing if you do that once more."

Unperturbed, Newton went past ten minutes the next week. At twelve and a half minutes, Reverend Clippenberger stood up and asked Newton to stop the record. Newton merely smiled and said, "It will be over soon." Angered, the pastor began his sermon with the music still playing.

That Sunday Newton slipped out before the service was over and was not seen all week. The next Sunday was normal. Newton played a five-minute hymn and stopped. The following week he played for five minutes again, but during the last twenty minutes of the service, strains of the fifth Beethoven symphony could be heard low over the amplifier.

"You're going to drive me crazy, Newton," said the pastor.

"Oh, you're too strong for that," said Newton. But for six weeks he gave Clippenberger a break. He must have been marshalling his forces. For at the end of the period, he attacked with a fifteen-minute selection by Michael Haydn. Then twenty minutes of Mozart, twenty-five of Handel, and a half hour of Moussorgsky.

Reverend Clippenberger threatened to resign. Newton backed off to fifteen minutes of Rameau. The following Sunday Newton didn't come to church at all. This made everyone nervous, even the pastor.

The end came six weeks before the visit by the short-haired jolly dresser to my door. During the whole sermon the "Emperor Concerto" played low over the amplifier. Newton left early again, and no one could find the turntable, so they couldn't turn it off.

The next week the music was playing even louder when everyone arrived. There were selections from Richard Strauss, Teleman, and Vivaldi. Again, they could not find the source, and Newton was absent. The third week the "Messiah" was beginning as the first churchgoers arrived and was so loud in places that the sermon was interrupted. Again, Newton could not be found.

Three weeks before the rude parishioner came to my house looking for Newton, the music was so loud that nothing else could be heard. The congregation had had to adjourn to the lawn. Now they were meeting at the schoolhouse.

Acoustics engineers had been called, but were sending for new, more sensitive equipment to locate the dozens of speakers that had been hidden over the building in such a way that the very walls vibrated, making accurate detection impossible. They had still not discovered the record player or the amplifier.

I was, of course, no help to the man. And I never saw Newton Abbot again. I heard that it took them two months to get the music out of the church and that to this day, they have not found the source. Newton's house is still dark and empty, a police investigation and search have turned up nothing. Reverend Clippenberger suffered a heart attack and retired, and a new minister who believes in folk masses and guitar music has come to preach.

Grenada 1967

From my spot on the side of the mountain I can see down through the foliage to the coast and the beach and the ocean just beyond. It is a long way to the water, more than three miles, but on this day the westward-blowing winds have lifted the mists and cleared the air. And even as they have carried the saline richness of the ocean up the slopes they seem to have carried in their warm and swirling thermals the sights and sounds of the ocean and the gently rising hills between us. For all things are clearer. I hear, like a whisper, the breakers crash upon the shore. A whisper, but I hear it nonetheless. And the faint rolling lines of white are visible above the troughs which they follow onto the beach. I imagine and feel their splashing hissing collapse on the sandy shore. And I wonder, in my labors, if these same waves have come to break before me, all the way from Africa or Europe.

The bananas are heavy, and despite the rolled banana-leaf pad that protects the crown of my head, they bump and chaff my scalp. I have fallen twice today, both times in the rocky stream just before the road, and cut one leg and bruised the other. The paths between the banana plants are slick this morning from the rain in the night, and our bare feet have churned it into a sticky paste. Because of the moisture, there is also a greater danger of spiders and snakes, and we are all just slightly nervous today. The winds blowing up and over the old volcano are part of a high-pressure system that is moving in after the rain, and they are chilly. We are wearing ragged sweaters or extra jackets, and our movement is restricted in the heavy garments.

Four of us have already finished nearly a quart of rough white rum even though we have only been carrying since six this morning and it is not yet ten. The rum, carried down our throats by a glass of water, warms our bellies and evaporates, like a spirit, out through our limbs, stirring them. Except when we find a banana plant blown down by a storm or fallen limb, one which has gone unnoticed and therefore ripened naturally, or one of us scales a coconut palm for milky nuts, there is nothing to eat. There isn't time, for the bunches of bananas, called *figs* in this unripe state, must be carried down to the lorry and loaded carefully on beds of banana leaves. We then haul them down a narrow road to the packing shed, where toothless old women cull and trim the bunches, paint the ends to prevent them from bleeding and pack them in plastic bags which come off a long seemingly endless roll near the ceiling. The banana boat comes only on Tuesday, so we must prepare on Monday, all the *figs* we wish to send. At eight tonight we will finish, and then we will eat.

Going back up the hill I step over one of the drainage ditches that lace the banana plots and meet Jack coming down with three bunches on his head. As always, Jack is smiling. He is a large copper-colored man, tall and strong, and his feet are the largest I have ever seen, their natural length having been enhanced by the splaying effect of a lifetime without shoes. Jack is somewhere between twenty-five and fifty years old, and there are only blackened stumps of teeth in his mouth. He is a strong but gentle man, who laughs quickly and deeply, humor rippling through his whole body. I will miss Jack.

The reason I have fallen is because of my excitement. I have long learned to walk the water-slick stones in the stream, to sweat out the harsh rum, and to go without the three meals a day. I am healthier for it. My arms and legs are stronger, and so is my neck and my back. My neck is stronger from carrying bananas, but my back is strong because of Marie. She is my reason for being here right now, and my reason for leaving, and I will miss her. My excitement is bittersweet. I will be gone in two days, and my mind wanders as it has not done for months now, and I slip on the wet stones.

Further up the slope, Marie's father, Big Johnny, is choosing mature *figs* and cutting them with his machete. As I come up to lift another bunch, he shouts to me, "Mind my *figs*, Boon boy. You fall two times today. You want woman work in the shed? Walk softly, you hear?"

"Yes, Big Johnny," I say. "No problem." I hunker down, and Charlie, Marie's brother, positions a large bunch on my head, balancing it perfectly on the rolled pad of leaves. I push up and glide off down the slope, arms and legs swinging from an erect and perfectly straight torso which carries the weight down to the hips. These plots are far up on the side of the mountain, near the top of the dead volcano. The volcano has been silent for many years now, and its slopes are thickly forested, and cultivated vegetables or wild vines grow equally well in the deep lava soil that formed on the hills and across the plateau at the base of the mountain. Everything is green here always and moist, for it is either raining or the jungle is sweating out the water in its pores. Except on rare days like this one, we move in thick air, and a kind of steamy mist hangs in the top of the trees and floats upon the ridges.

Here and there, giant rocks loom up out of the earth's surface like monuments, dark and brooding, pitched at crazy angles. Between the ridges, the streams flow over beds filled with large black stones, so there are few smooth cascades or still pools but rather a noisy rush of spills and splashes as the water fights its way down to the ocean.

As I make my way down to the lorry on the road far below, I am glad that this last day on the slopes is such a clear and vibrant one, for these are the memories that will live in me the longest and my senses are already supremely aware of all that is happening around me.

In spite of the rum, my mind is focused and keen, and my anticipation of leaving is balanced against memories of the last six months on the island. It was only last night that I knew for sure that

I would be able to leave, and so there has not been much time for remembering. There will be time enough for that later. For now, the past and future images crowd me, and I can't think of them all at once. I drift.

* * * *

I came to the island on a sailing boat, one of the yachts that makes its way up and down the Windward and Leeward Islands, frequently having arrived from Europe by way of the Canary Islands off Africa. Our second night in the harbor we went ashore to find drink, women, a dance, or perhaps all three. There were three of us, the crew of the *Mary Lee*, which sailed charters out of Charlotte Amalie in the Virgin Islands. We were on our way south to pick up a family from Barbados. At the first seaside bar, we learned that a dance hall south of the town and on the beach had a live band on Saturday nights and that the ratio of women to men was very favorable. We hailed a taxi, and he took us there.

The dance hall was built on stilts, and the beat of the calypso band filtered down from the dance floor long before we reached the steps that led up to it. The night was hot, and behind us the music echoed back from the trees and bush, soggy and muted, with a kind of swaying tropical indolence. Beyond the hall was the beach, and low waves played along the shore, the lights from the building rising and falling in shimmering cadence with the tossing water.

In the hall itself, drinks were cheap, the music was good, and there were more lovely women than a person could count. By eleven, our captain, who called himself Sly, had become drunk on Rusty Nails, fallen in the ocean, been rescued, gotten sick, and finally, had dropped off to sleep by one of the stilts holding up the dancehall. Eddie, the mate and cook, had found a "friend" and gone off to her cabin for the rest of the night. I had danced with innumerable women but had not seized upon one that I wished to spend the night with. The reason was this: at a table at the edge of the dance floor, seated between two men, was the most beautiful darker-skinned girl I had seen in any place, at any time up to that point. She was slightly stout of hip and larger-breasted, but her face was delicate and lovely. She wasn't overweight, just nicely rounded and very firm looking, if that description makes sense, and I found her ridiculously appealing. But because of the presence of her male friends, I was reluctant to ask her to dance, so I merely looked from time to time.

She occasionally glanced back. As the evening wore on, I noticed that when she did dance, it was only with one of the two men who were seated with her. No one else approached her.

A good calypso band, plenty of cheap rum, and a hot night in the Caribbean will go a long way to removing inhibitions and shyness, social customs that have been built up in a lifetime of training. At a little after eleven I went to her table and asked to buy the three of them a drink. They accepted. I sat down, and we began to talk. They were very friendly, and their English was excellent. They were most interested in the fact that I was an American. After about twenty minutes I asked the men collectively if they would allow me to ask the lady to dance, one dance only if they pleased. They agreed, and she seemed pleased to have been asked so politely. We walked to the floor and began to dance close together to the slowest thing a calypso band is capable of.

"These men, they are your fiancé and a friend, no doubt," I suggested as we danced.

She laughed, "Oh no. They are my brothers."

"But I notice that no one else asks you to dance, and certainly that is not because you are not attractive. You are the most beautiful woman here tonight."

She laughed. "That's a nice compliment. But you see, my father is a very famous man on this island, and I think really that some of these people are afraid of me."

"Why is your father so famous?"

"Oh, no particular reason, he just is." I later learned that a person should pay attention to such short answers to such short questions.

"I suppose that I am very lucky to have this chance to dance with you then."

"Oh, yes, and you may dance with me more this evening if you wish. I would prefer that."

I was pleased to hear her say that, and I spent the rest of the evening with her, dancing with no one else. Her brothers had drifted away from the table now and danced occasionally with girls whom they seemed to know. A little after two in the morning, as the band was playing the last number of the night, she said to me, "Would you be pleased to come with me?"

I replied, "Yes."

"Good, we have a car outside. My brothers will drive."

She led me to the car, and she and I got into the back seat of a large sedan along with one of the brothers and a girl he had met at the dance hall. With so many people, it meant that the girls had to sit mostly on our laps. The other brother was in the front seat with a young woman also. I was too drunk to note the direction in which we were travelling, and the girl, whose name was Marie, had become affectionate in the darkness of the car, even with the closeness of the brothers and the two other girls.

I was aware that the car climbed a mountain for some time and then descended, but I had no idea where we were. After nearly an hour, during which time I had been held securely by Marie, the car drew up between two tall palm trees, and I realized we were at a beach that must be on the opposite side of the island from the capital city and the dance hall.

Nearby, there was a house built like the dance hall, on stilts, and dim yellow light shone through the closed shutters. The two brothers and their girls headed for the house, and I stumbled out of the car and tried to follow. I was brought up short by Marie, who said, "There is not enough room for all of us there. You come with me."

We walked out onto the beach and further south out of the glow of the lights from the little beach house. I said to her, "I don't have a bathing suit."

"Neither do I," she said. "That is okay."

We disrobed on the beach and walked into the water. The nicest thing about the Caribbean waters is their warmth, and especially at night, when the air has taken on a chill, they seem to surround and hold you like a mother's womb.

We swam and floated near the shore, in a kind of expectant ritual, touching occasionally but not for long. At last, as if by signal, we made our way to the soft beach beyond the water's edge, and now, instead of floating on the slowly rolling waves that washed in across the gently rising sand, we floated instead in a rhythmic duet with its own rolling sweeping waves.

Just before dawn, Marie led me to the beach house where there was an extra room after all, and we climbed into a bed on the beach side of the house and fell asleep.

A few hours later, mid-morning by the feel of the light streaming into the room, I woke up, and Marie was still asleep beside me, but we were no longer alone. Seated by the door were three men, two of them older, perhaps in their fifties and one of the brothers from last night. He had a machete on his lap. The faces all resembled each other.

I shook Marie awake and drew the sheet tighter against my body. She blinked awake, sat up, and said, "Oh, hi Papa, hi Uncle," and pulled her shift on under the cover, slipped out of the bed, and disappeared.

I looked from face to face, found my trousers by the bed, made great work of putting them on, and stood up to leave the room. The brother with the machete blocked the door.

"I really need to use the bathroom," I said.

"No problem. I'll come with you. Then Papa needs to talk to you."

"Hey, I'm sorry if…"

"Don't talk. Come. It's this way."

He led me to a small toilet, where I relieved myself while he waited outside the door. He then escorted me back to the bedroom where I had spent the last few hours. Papa and Uncle were still there. I want to believe that I was mostly sober by that time, given the time Marie and I had spent in the water and the few hours of sleep. Looking back the series of events do have a dreamlike quality to them, however.

"So, you like my daughter, do you?" said Papa, the man I would come to know as Big Johnny.

"Yes, sir. She is a very nice girl, very pretty."

"Do you always seduce nice, pretty girls as soon as you meet them? Is that how they do things in America?"

"I'm sorry, but I don't think that's exactly how things happened," I said, not sure what response would keep the machete safely away from my limbs and neck. The brother was smiling. "I thought…"

"Ah, you thought. Thinking is not good enough sometimes. Sometimes you have to ask and talk and be sure about things. Anyway, no problem, my daughter likes you, I think, so you can marry her this afternoon. You don't just come here and take advantage of peoples' daughters and then just abandon them. No, no, it is not the island way, it is not the Big Johnny way."

"But don't I get to talk to Marie about this first?" I asked, trying to buy time. "This seems awfully rushed, and I have a commitment to the rest of the crew on the boat."

"Don't worry about that. We have spoken to them. They were not in very good shape this morning, and they will miss you, but they will find someone to take your place. You can talk to Marie, but let me just tell you how it is going to be. You are actually a very lucky young man. You will like it here. No winters like in America. A secure place in my family. And such a lovely wife. She has always been a good daughter to me. She has even been to school in England."

He puffed himself up. "I have prepared her well. She knows how to talk to you better than I can. I can talk to you good, but I still have many island manners of speaking that I will never forget or change. Marie is not so. She will talk to you good. And she has the body of a good mother. Wide hips like her mama. You are lucky to know such a woman."

He stood up. "Now you can talk to Marie, but only for a minute. You must get ready. You will marry her this afternoon. It will be very nice."

With that, he and the other two men left the room, and he called to Marie, who appeared a few moments later, still in her shift, but with her face washed and hair combed. She was as alluring as she had been the night before, but I needed to get myself out of this mess.

"Marie, what the heck is going on? He says I have to marry you this afternoon. I don't even know you. This is crazy."

She laughed. "Just go along with it, okay. Don't you like me? You liked me last night."

"Of course I like you. You are fun and beautiful, but usually you get to know a girl a bit before you marry her, and the girl gets to know the guy a bit. Maybe I'm a lazy useless boat guy who drinks too much and has no money."

"Papa will take care of that. You get to work for him. He doesn't care how much you drink as long as you can work."

"You're serious."

She laughed again. "And you get me. We are going to have a good time. This is a great place to live. Much better than England. I didn't like it there at all. I have to go get ready now. So do you. Give me a kiss."

She kissed me lightly on the mouth, which must have taken courage given that I hadn't brushed my teeth yet, and left the room.

The brother, whose name was Little Johnny, reappeared, and he had with him my duffel bag from the *Mary Lee* with my toiletries and some clean clothes. "You need to get cleaned up, then we will fit you with some clothes for the wedding. Go take a shower. I will wait for you. And shave."

He handed me the bag and pushed me toward the bathroom.

* * * *

The wedding took place that afternoon in the garden behind a house that Marie's family lived in further up the mountain. I was dressed in a fine suit that someone in the village had loaned to the family for just this occasion. An older lady friend had altered it on a hand-driven sewing machine in my presence, an hour or two earlier. I wore a pair of Little Johnny's shoes, which fit when newspaper was stuffed in the toes.

But Marie had to undergo no such adjustment to her clothes. Her dress was long and flowing and made of the finest material. She carried a lovely bouquet of tropical flowers, and she was radiantly beautiful. The best man was Little Johnny, but his real role was to keep me in line. He had a small but very serviceable pistol tucked in his belt. After my short discussion with Marie earlier, my opinion was not asked about anything.

The wedding night was magnificent. There is no other way to describe it. I became a bit tipsy immediately after the wedding vows were finalized and floated in that tropical garden behind Marie's father's house until all of the guests had gone home, and Marie and I were finally shown to our own room. I had drunk perhaps a hundred toasts during the afternoon and pledged a thousand allegiances to a family I knew nothing about and had separated myself completely from the world which I had known. I felt that I was merely a participant in a long and drunken dream.

But as we undressed in the second floor bedroom of her father's house, with a lazy fan stirring insects above us, the jungle singing, swishing, and chattering beyond the double open doors that led onto the balcony, and as her brother's shadow grew and diminished on the frosted glass door that separated us from the hallway, I began to realize that no dream is so long or so vivid. At first, I was afraid. But then, I looked at the beautiful light brown and smiling girl who revealed herself so gladly to me, and the presence of her brother outside the room became protective, the jungle became friendly, and for a few moments I understood all that had happened in the past twenty-four hours and let myself be embraced by it.

At six the following morning, I was called from the marriage bed and led to the banana plots above the house and the village. Little Johnny molded my first banana-leaf pad for me and put a small bunch of bananas on my head. "You are a member of a banana family now. You must learn all there is to know."

I carried bananas the whole of that day and became high before noon on the rum we drank.

That was a Monday. On Tuesday, I helped load the bananas on the lorry, and we took them down to the wharf in St. Georges, the capital. On Wednesday, we dug holes for the new banana plants and filled them with natural compost. On Thursday we trimmed suckers from the older plants and planted them in the newly dug holes. On Friday, we gardened or picked up nutmeg and stripped the bright red plastic-looking cover from the nuts. This was mace, and all of it would need to dry on racks. We took the separated spices down to the drying house and laid them out in wire-bottomed trays to dry. The drying house was built up from the ground so that the air could pass under it and up through the floor. At all hours of the day, the fresh sweet smell of the nutmeg would brush around us, and in the evening, it would drift like incense through the sleeping rooms on the second floor of the house. In spite of its being always with us, we never tired of it. Its wafting and waning were like scent notes in a tone poem.

Saturday was a market day, and occasionally we would prepare parcels to be taken down to St. Georges by the women, for sale there. There was not much work on Saturday, and frequently, in the evening, there was a dance in a local or nearby hall. Sunday was a sleepy day. Nothing was done except the cooking, a bit of drinking, and a great deal of resting and recovering from the dance or the party on the previous night. It was the only day of the week when one did not arise automatically with the sun or before it.

You may wonder that I could accept, so easily, such an initiation into a culture so greatly removed from the one I had known up to that point. If you knew me better or had had the opportunity to spend a week or two on the island, amongst the members of my newfound family, you might find my acceptance easier to understand. I am a very easygoing individual who accepts most generally that which is given me, and as long as it is not particularly odious, find something to redeem it. In this case, there was really, beyond a certain lack of freedom (which I scarcely noticed anyway; after all, how much freedom is there onboard a small sailing vessel which requires constant cleaning, minding, polishing, and sail trimming while tossing about?), there was nothing that I wanted for. There was a very solid roof over my head, the work was hard but pleasant, and it made me feel good. There was more than sufficient to drink, and the family, despite certain strange beliefs about courtship and marriage, were pleasant, humorous, and hearty people whom I quickly grew to like. After the first month there was no need to guard against my running away.

And there were two other things which made my early leaving improbable. One of those was the food. I have said that we ate only once per day. Essentially that is true. In the morning, we would drink a quick cup of strong coffee and eat whatever leftovers were there from the night before. During the day we existed on the rum and raw vegetables, bananas, or wild fruit. But in the evening, after our baths, we ate such meals as kings of old and those who live in the midst of plenty are accustomed to. Soups and stews which had simmered low over an open fire in a great iron pot, rich with dumplings, fish, and vegetables, were always served on Monday night. And all the family and those who had labored on the slopes and in the shed were there to eat it. There was rum and cold beer. On other days we ate fried green bananas or plantain stewed and sugared. There were sweet potatoes, a dozen kinds of yams, ripe green beans and peas, fat red tomatoes, and a multitude of other green vegetables which I had never heard of. There was chicken, fresh ocean fish, and from time to time, wild game from the forest on the far side of the mountain. My muscles became firm and strong.

But more important than the food was Marie, my pistol and machete bride. I must admit that for several days after the forced wedding I bore some hard feelings toward her and her family. (This was after the effects of the rum had evaporated, usually in the very early morning hours.) I felt that they had been somewhat callous and nonchalant in handling the whole affair, having not taken much account of my own potential interests.

But Marie was so nice to me, as if she felt some slight guilt for my forced position as a husband. She fussed about me like a mother hen, making sure I was well fed, keeping my limited supply of clothes washed and ironed, preparing me a bath in the evening, bringing cold beer for me to drink; there was no need that went unattended. And always, in the cool, spicy air of our bedroom, she drew me down to the golden-brown smoothness of her warmth, rocking me higher and higher, until, like an object thrown too far, I burst through gravity and showered myself into a million tiny pieces upon the sky.

I had been somewhat careless that first night on the beach, and on the following one, but after that, I spoke to Marie about pregnancy and protection. She laughed and told me that she had taken care of that and not to worry. In spite of what her father had said to me about her mothering attributes, she had no desire to have any children any time soon. Indeed, she had been in England for nursing school, it turned out, and she was still studying to take an exam to practice nursing in a local hospital on the island. I never could understand how a young woman with that much education and that much sense of purpose could allow her father to marry her off to a stranger after one night. Several weeks after the ceremony, I asked her if we were really married or if I had just misunderstood the event and it was just a welcoming party and a kind of joke. "Don't worry about it," she said. "I know you will leave some day. Just enjoy it for now."

All in all, there was little to complain about. For four months I lived in the village on the side of the mountain and visited occasionally the house on the beach, the one to which I had been brought on my first night with Marie. After the second month, I was allowed to drive the lorry which carried the bananas down to the wharf, and Marie and I would sometimes go out unescorted. Life was pleasant.

In the beginning of the fifth month, I began to feel, however, a certain longing to leave the village, a desire to be again my own person. I had never stayed so long in one place, and the rich life and the joys of Marie were beginning to pale. I wanted to read a western novel, talk to an American, hear a violin. So I began to try to arrange a departure. I found it simpler to think about than to do. Almost always, when I went down to St. Georges, I went with Marie, her father, or one of her brothers. And even when I went alone, there was not always a yacht in the harbor which I might approach. Several yacht owners with whom I finally did talk had no need for extra bodies on their small ships.

But eventually, near the end of the sixth month, I found a yacht short of help for the passage back up through the islands and on to Miami. Onboard were two early-to-middle-aged men, their younger wives, and a still younger mate or part-time captain. I met only with the owner, one of the men, by chance, in a bar near the center of town on banana day. I told him of my predicament, attested to my ability to sail, and was shown the sleek vessel the next week when I came down with bananas again. The rest of the party had gone ashore, so I didn't meet them. They were planning to leave on the following Wednesday, the day after the banana boat came, which suited me fine. He agreed to circle the island and to send a dinghy into the shore to pick me up at midnight. On Sunday we met outside the village, reviewed the plan, shook hands on it, and parted. I still had only met the owner.

I had resolved when I decided to leave the island not to think about the time I had spent there until I was gone. I had never fully questioned Marie and her family's abduction of me. Surely their reasons were good. And they had treated me quite well. I didn't want any feelings of remorse or regret to come between me and my decision to leave, for I knew, deep within it was the right choice to leave now. Indeed, hadn't Marie said that she knew I would leave sometime? I wondered if I might have not been the first husband to that lovely woman.

* * * *

Which brings me back to today and the weight of the bananas on my head. By noon, the air has warmed, and we shed our sweaters and jackets. We continue to carry bananas until nearly dark for the wind and the rains that have just passed have knocked down many plants and we must try to salvage as many bananas as we can.

So many bunches means that the women in the packing shed will be far behind, and we will work late, past ten tonight. Sure enough, it is nearly midnight when the last *figs* are wrapped and sealed and we set off down the slope to have our dinner.

It is usually a good soup that we are served this night, with ocean Jacks, short broad fish that are cleaned and then cooked whole in the broth. The dumplings are large and light, and we all eat heartily. Despite my promise to avoid reflection, I realize that this is probably my last stew on the island. Regret grows like a pain in my middle, and long before I am full, I cease eating. Marie notices but says nothing. Later when we are alone together, I make every effort to please her.

In the morning, we are all sluggish as we load the lorry, and it takes longer than normal. Big Johnny is in a bad mood today, but he says nothing. Even Jack seems tired. On the wharf, there is a long line of trucks, everyone having extra bananas because of the storm.

As I sit at the wheel, I can see, way down the wharf, the man on whose yacht I am to ship tomorrow night. From his face I can tell that he is looking for someone, and I am sure that someone is me. "I need to piss," I say to Big Johnny's man beside me. "Move the truck if I am not back when the line moves." He frowns at my use of the American term for lorry, but slides into the driver's seat, proud of the responsibility. I hope he knows how to drive.

I slide between the waiting lorries, out of sight of in-laws and others I have grown to know. And when I am abreast of the old man, I signal to him. He ducks through and starts to speak, but I raise my hand in warning. Beyond the perimeter of the long open-sided shed, we pause in the shadow of the scale house. "We are leaving tonight." This is a day earlier than we had agreed to. He says it with a straight face, but I feel a guilty smile below the surface.

"But you said you were leaving tomorrow night."

"We finished provisioning early."

"Provisioning? How many provisions do you need for an island-to-island hop up to Miami?"

"Well, you never know. Things are cheaper here than on some of the other islands."

This is difficult. Tomorrow night Marie would have been away with her girlfriends. Tonight I will have to slip out with a good excuse or without her knowing.

"Alright, I'll be ready. Same place?"

"Yes. Same spot we discussed."

He slips out behind the shed, and I walk back to the lorry. It has moved twice. Across the wharf, the banana boat, which is actually a fairly large ocean-going ship, is taking on bananas through four doors which open out on the side at the level of the dock. The ship is white and looks clean and freshly painted. The are four red electric conveyors carrying the plastic-wrapped bunches of bananas into the ship, and they resemble foggy mollusks parading into the interior of the vessel. Inside the ship, huge sweating black men in little more than loincloths take the bunches from the conveyors and pack them in slatted wooden bunks for the long voyage to England. It is hot inside the ship, and the one time I went to look inside the door, the man inside swore at me and threatened to neuter me.

At last, we unload and leave, climbing the green hills above St. Georges with its sheltered harbor and tiered rows of colorful houses and the great white ship gleaming with metal brightness by the wharf.

Throughout the afternoon, sadness grows like sleep, rising from the very soles of my feet, whispering regret and tugging like a shadow the warmth from existence. A character in a book about the post-colonial world in Nigeria said once, "things fall apart." But it is also true that things fall together sometimes, for I had landed, like a seed on the wind, in a fertile place and flourished there. I had known happiness and a form of love. I had breathed the island mists and inhaled its spices and had likewise given back, in labor and sweat, a part of myself. I was certain though that the place held no permanence for me, and despite my regrets, I knew I would leave.

At ten, after eating, I tell Marie that I am going out for a walk, which I sometimes do. I am wearing clean shorts and shirt and have some money with me, and that is all I will take.

"Don't wait up for me," I say to Marie, and kiss her lightly as I leave. It is necessary to rush out of the house.

The cove is over four miles away by path, I reach it just before midnight. The yacht is lying out some distance, beyond a close reef at the mouth of the cove. I stand on the beach for a long minute and finally signal with a small flashlight. A small dinghy sets out from the yacht's side and comes in for me. "What, you have brought nothing with you?" says the man who I have been meeting with.

"It was not possible on this short notice." I am irritated that he asked. It is his fault.

When we reach the yacht, I climb up and help him and the other man bring up the dinghy and lash it onto the foredeck. We go aft and he starts the diesel and sets the autopilot. I sit on a seat at the stern and watch the lights of this island recede as we make our way out to deeper water for a safe passage around the island. The island starts to fade away in a mist of time and memory, and at last I allow the full weight of my sadness do some creeping, and it almost crushes me. We turn gently toward the north. After a brief introduction to the vessel, one I am familiar with from other passages, I am assigned to be on watch, as we are only motoring because of a light breeze. The rest of the passengers on the boat seem to be asleep.

At four, one of the men comes up to relieve me, and the other takes me below to show me my cabin. In the dim light I can see that there is already someone asleep in the bed, which is narrower than a normal double bed. I step back into the corridor. "There must be a mistake, there is someone already in there."

"Oh no, no mistake. That is my wife's sister. She's divorced, but a very charming woman. She saw you on the dock."

"Wait a minute…"

"Well, there's always the floor, but it's hard." He replied.

I stare at him, bewildered.

"Oh, yes," he goes on, "there is one other thing. We have changed our plans slightly. We are heading to Bermuda and on to the Azores and Spain now that we have someone with your experience onboard. I hope that won't inconvenience you too much."

He disappears into his cabin and shuts the door.

Humor of God

Each morning, he stakes two cans of cold beer from the refrigerator and drives to the highest hill on the farm. Looking out across the farm and the valley beyond, he arranges, in his mind, the day before him. He never goes alone. The four beagles and the labrador, like the tail on the kite, always follow. When he stops the truck the dogs range out across the field, little antennae, testing the morning for him, and sending back, in howls and yips, synaptic bursts of information. In twenty-five years, he has learned to forecast the weather by the carrying of noises in the morning air. He is more frequently right than the weather station in town.

This morning is a clear one. The sun breaks, like water, over the mountain to the east, the warm light falling first through the gaps and hollows into the valley beyond. Given body by the rising mists, the sunlight slides across the landscape toward him, defining elevations, poking and stirring the earth into life.

Below him, in the house, blue smoke rises from the chimney in a straight line, then, deprived of life, billows out in a small pale cloud above the homestead. It is a still morning.

In the house, the two women will be cooking breakfast on the old wood stove. They claim that the food tastes better prepared on the old cast top of the Range Eternal that has stood before the chimney for fifty years. The flat black top extends across the whole stove and above it is the warming oven. To the right is a water jacket. It is a good stove, efficient in every sense, and the women are right. The food from it is better if only because the wood—the oak, the pine, the wild cherry, the maple occasionally—are products of his own labor. Sawn and quartered, wedged and split, the splined, barkless sticks glow and melt in the tiny firebox. Cooking is a ritual.

After the beers he returns to the house, trailing beagles. Before he reaches the kitchen, the smells come to greet him—sausage, scrapple, potatoes, apples. Breakfast is no mean affair here. There will also be eggs, biscuits, coffee, applesauce, and probably ham or chicken. And two fingers of vodka for himself. He believes that the vodka will make him live longer.

He will eat two meals today. Today the Reverend Brother Kline is to call on him. It is now close on ten years since he set foot in a church, but the church has not, in its mercy, abandoned him. He knows for the what the Reverend is coming today, and it amuses him. At breakfast he mentions the visit.

"I prefer to receive the Reverend alone, if you don't mind." It was more a question than a statement.

"As you wish. I have no truck with him." It is Martha, the eldest of the women who speaks first.

"Shall we send in tea or coffee?" Maggie who is younger makes the suggestion.

"Send tea for the Reverend and vodka for me. In a plain glass."

Martha says, "You will taunt him, whatever, won't you?" It is not said bitterly.

"It is his position to be taunted. It enhances his character. And his salary," he smiles.

It has been a full year since Maggie's husband died. A first heart attack debilitated him, and a second one took him. It is Maggie's house which they all share. Before the death of Maggie's husband, he and Martha held the farm next door, and the two families traded only labor. Now he is the master of both properties, and of both women. It is that that the minister is coming about. He will quote scripture, Old Testament and New, and will seek to extract a comment. In that, it will be a waste of the minister's time.

Once before, six months after the death of Maggie's husband, a deputation of Christians had come to visit. Five men had been sent to discuss his unusual style of living. It was felt in the small community that he was a bad influence on the children, for the gossip circulated at all levels. He had always been unusual but this last was beyond the ability of the community to accept. The five men, farmers all, had been received by Petersen and the two women in the most cordial of manners. They had served tea, then vodka, then dandelion wine. The men had sat on their hands until the vodka came, and after that they had lost sight of their visit's purpose. They had gone away drunk, and Petersen had achieved a new level of decadence in the eyes of the community. Two days later the wife of one of the men had accosted him at the feed store. He had stood smiling as she upbraided him for drugging her husband, a deacon.

Then she had said, "The Good Lord himself only knows what you are capable of, Mr. Petersen."

At that Petersen opened his eyes wide, fared his nostrils, breathed in deeply, and exhaled like a bull, swaying on his sturdy legs. The woman had clasped her hand to her mouth and fled. No other wives complained to him.

When Maggie's husband had died it had been only natural that the farms were consolidated. Maggie's husband had been Petersen's half-brother, and Petersen's wife Martha was Maggie's sister. Maggie's house was the better of the two, so he and Martha moved to the better place. Petersen did not know if the two women had discussed it beforehand, but on the first night, Maggie had said, "You will be husband to us both now. I could not stand to find another man." And so the three of them had come to sleep in one bed, Petersen between the two women. They had put two beds together side by side, and stitched up quilts and blankets to match.

That facet of the relationship had been discovered by accident when the house had been repainted just after Petersen and Martha moved in. John Claytor had come to paint early one morning and had seen the three of them in bed together. He had slipped away from the upstairs porch window unnoticed but had spread the word. Cecil, Petersen's closest friend had asked him outright if the three of them slept together. Petersen merely said, "It would save fuel in the winter, wouldn't it?" Despite probing, Petersen would say no more. The sisters were attractive, and he knew that more than Christian outrage prompted the questions.

Today, however, none of these things were on his mind. He lived his life with the steady resolution that he alone was responsible for his decisions, and once made they were behind him. If he was morally blighted, so be it. The community could stand it. His ostracism was odd in one respect, for no stronger link existed in that invisible chain than sustained the people in this rural place. His help was offered and received with good cheer, and from time to time his polygamous leanings were forgotten.

At two the minister arrived. He was a slightly stocky man, the product of too many Sunday dinners and not enough hard labor. He had written two years' worth of sermons when he first became preacher, and now, in his fiftieth year, he was well into the fifteenth repetition. Petersen knew that. And being a clever, curious, and sometimes goading individual, he had mentioned it to the Reverend during the third cycle. The Reverend had disclaimed it, but Petersen knew better and took every opportunity to remind him of it.

"Well, well, Brother Kline, it's nice of you to come by. We haven't seen you for a long time. Let's see, you should be up to the Sins of Isaac by now, shouldn't you? Or is it Esau? No, no. That sermon was called The Sins of Isaac, and then you jumped ahead of Psalms and did a special series for Thanksgiving. And then of course it was the Christmas season. You see, Brother Kline, I probably followed your sermons more closely than anyone else at the church. Aren't you pleased with that? Although, really, don't you think you should update the material a little?"

"Brother Petersen, the word of God does not need updating; it is always the same. And I fear that though the message remains nearly the same, it does not produce the desired change in the listener. Do you see my point?"

"Clearly, clearly, Brother Kline, and I say to you that I am pleased to have a man as busy as yourself take time to visit a man like myself with his little sins."

"And are they so little, Brother Petersen?"

"Ah, I certainly hope so. I do from time to time exceed Anstie's limit in my consumption of alcohol, but never do I become a less than honorable creature under its effect, and I believe that is proper behavior, don't you?"

"It is not my position to describe proper behavior; that is God's prerogative alone. I am only sent as a reminder, a burr if you will, although I prefer the image our Master gave us, which is that of the Divine Shepherd."

"Brother Kline, I'm glad you mentioned that. It is something I've been wanting to talk to you about for a long time, and I never got around to it. Don't you find it just slightly disturbing that the images in Christianity are so...what?...agrarian, so agricultural in nature? You know, this whole business of sheep and the flock, really, I don't find myself warming to the concept at all. In fact, I find it just slightly demeaning to be compared to a sheep, which as you may or may not know, is one of the dumbest animals in the world. They're not even graceful."

"Brother Petersen, I fear that you take this symbolism too lightly, that you use it as a mere toy, a plaything for your admittedly superior intellect. That in and of itself displays to me a certain callousness, a certain elite attitude, a certain sinful sense of superiority. Don't you see my point? Just because you can grasp the proper relationship between the Divine Trinity and those of us who are so lowly that we inhabit this earth, doesn't mean that all men can do so. Those divinely inspired souls who brought the word of God to us through the Bible knew in their God-granted wisdom that most men needed to be reassured and placed, at the same time, in their proper position in the universe. What better way than to use imagery that all men could understand? Never forget, Brother Petersen, that you were born into sin, and if Christ had not come to this earth and perished, you would die in sin. You are not as well off as sheep. I find it surprising that you object to being compared to a sheep. If I might say so, I believe that it is the sheep that has the right to feel offended."

"Remarkable, truly remarkable, Brother Kline. The last remark reveals to me a side of your character hitherto completely unknown. Remarkable. You are a man of rare humor, really and truly. Tell me, Brother Kline, do you think God has a sense of humor?"

"Brother Petersen I'm not sure that your question doesn't border on the blasphemous."

"Oh, come now, Brother Kline, surely you don't mean that. It would be an awfully petty deity who couldn't be asked whether he had a sense of humor, don't you think? Really, I think that any mind that is broad-reaching simply must have a sense of humor. And we do agree that the intellect of God has to be broadest reaching of all minds, don't we? Of course we do. You are a manifestation of that belief, and even I, who rejects the institution, embrace some of the beliefs. And, even I, no, especially I, believe that God has a sense of humor. No. I will say it even more firmly. I *know* that God has a sense of humor. I am proof of it."

"How so?"

"Well now, that I will not tell you. But there is one way that you may find out. If I precede you in death, you *may* know. Probably you will. So, my advice to you is to live a long, clean life, and a small bit of God's wisdom will be revealed to you. Not wisdom really, but humor, and that is sometimes wisdom in itself."

"For all that you are evil in the eyes of God, you are an interesting man, Brother Petersen. But I fear for your soul. And there are things that I must discuss with you. It is my duty as the servant of the Lord."

"No. There is nothing to discuss. The Lord has seen to all that I do. There is nothing for you to do. You have come because there are two women here, and you believe that both of them are wives to me. But there is nothing to discuss. They are under my protection, and that is all. What the community believes is up to the community. Besides, don't you think this community needs something to enliven it? Farming may be virtuous, but it becomes quite uninteresting at times, Brother Kline. I feel that I'm doing the community a service, really. Now there is more to discuss than the price of wheat. And since it is presumed to be a human failing, that makes it so much the more interesting. Don't you agree? I hope so."

"Brother Petersen…"

"No, there will be no more talk. I am glad you came today. It is good to talk to someone who is a good and challenging conversationalist, but I have now my work to do. The ladies will show you out when you have finished your tea. Good day."

And with that, Petersen arose and left the house. He felt no rancor for he had enjoyed the conversation, and the mildness of his spirit did not often admit anger.

In the evening, the preacher's visit was alluded to only briefly at supper, and then the talk turned to repair of fences and the need to prepare the windows for winter.

At bedtime, Petersen slipped into the bed first, having bathed earlier, as was the tradition. The women would come soon. Just before falling asleep, Petersen felt between his legs for the long thin weal of a scar that covered the place where his testicles had been before the landmine in Germany had torn them away nearly thirty years before. In peace, he smiled to himself.

Barcelona

Several weeks ago, while traveling in Spain, where I'm doing research on the Moorish influence on Spanish culture, I was able to obtain the last table at one of my favorite restaurants in Barcelona. I had not expected to be in the city that evening, and it was only due to an apparent late cancellation that I was able to be accommodated.

The restaurant is located to the north of the Passeig de Gracia, so tourists seldom happen onto it. It is charmingly laid out with comfortable armchairs and loveseats, and large pots of ferns and other flora provide separation and privacy for the diners.

My table was a smaller one for two and was just to the left when one entered, opposite the long bar on the right and shielded by one of the large ferns. It would have been a great place to have dinner with a lover.

I had just ordered a glass of Albariño and a bottle of agua con gas and was looking over the menu when I overheard a conversation between the maître d' and a man who had just stepped into the restaurant. The conversation was in English, and the person who had just come in appeared to be in the same situation in which I had found myself. He had no reservation but was hoping to dine there.

I would normally have ignored the conversation and counted myself fortunate at having snagged the table and left it at that. But something in the tone of the man's voice, his polite eloquence as he spoke to the maître d', and something in his slightly accented English drew me in. Just as the maître d' expressed his regrets for the second time for turning the gentleman away, I rose from the table and spoke to them both.

"Excuse me. I apologize, but I couldn't help but overhear your conversation. I wouldn't object to sharing my table this evening." I nodded to the man, who was dressed in expensive European-cut grey slacks and a light-colored linen jacket over a pale blue dress shirt. "I was in the same predicament just a moment ago."

"I don't want to intrude. I should have planned ahead," said the gentleman.

The maître d' looked at me. "Are you quite sure?"

"It's fine, please. I've been buried in books and research papers all day. Company would be welcome."

With that, he nodded, and the maître d' signaled to a waiter and pulled out the seat for my new dining companion.

"This is very kind of you. My name is Georj," he said, extending his hand, which I shook.

"I am Sebastian," I replied and motioned to the empty seat.

A waiter appeared, and Georj ordered a Dubonnet on ice, a drink that has apparently fallen out of favor in the US.

"Have you just arrived in Barcelona?" I asked, after he had ordered.

"Yes, but I know the city well. I come here often. And yourself?"

"I just came up from the south today, but I've spent a lot of time here. I like Barcelona better than Madrid, I think."

I had anticipated that he might then ask me where I was from, although it would have been evident from my accent that I was from the US or Canada. I was curious as to his origins but took a cue from his lack of asking and did not inquire.

"You mentioned research, I believe? Into what field? Art, history?" he said.

"Yes, as a matter of fact. I'm fascinated by the contributions of the Moors to Spanish history—how or whether that relates to the so-called golden age of Islam, which predates the Moors here, of course."

"Is that a personal interest, or do you teach on this subject? Are you a professor?"

"Not in a real sense," I replied. "I sold my business and dedicate my time to being a dilettante, dabbling in things that interest me."

"What a luxury."

"Yes, I suppose so. And you, what brings you to Barcelona?"

"I own a shoe business in Hungary, which I inherited from my father. I'm from further east, but I travel throughout Europe." He paused. "But on this trip, I'm here to put some family matters in order and to close a mental chapter putting thoughts of a troublesome episode behind me." He paused. "May I speak frankly about something that might disturb you?"

That question was open-ended and intriguing enough to generate a positive response on my part. "Of course."

"I killed a man two days ago."

"I'm sorry, did I hear that correctly?"

"Yes. I killed my uncle. It had to be done."

"Jesus! Should you be telling me this?" I wasn't sure how to react. A normal reaction might have been to laugh and to doubt what he had just said. But he had said it in such seriousness and with such an open look on his face, that I believed him.

"I don't know that it matters," he said, smiling. "Not that I mean to insult you by that comment. But I won't tell you where I'm from, and you won't see me again after this evening, I don't imagine. And if you were to ask the waiter to summon the local police, I would just say you misheard me, and it would all be embarrassing, and we might miss a nice dinner."

I studied his face for a moment and then laughed. "I'm not insulted. And I do believe you. But this strikes me as something a person would read in a novel."

He smiled once more. "A Russian one, most likely. But then the outcome for you might be less benign."

I laughed again, surprised at my comfort with the conversation. "Undoubtedly. So why are you telling me this? Am I to be your confessor?"

"Oh God, no. I have no guilt. This is not even an exercise in catharsis. I said I wanted to close a mental chapter. There *is* that. And I just want to put one regret behind me and close the book. But otherwise, it is more of a celebratory exercise."

"One regret? Do you regret killing this person who you said needed killing, or at least in so many words?"

"No, no, my regret is in not doing it sooner."

A waiter now approached and asked to take our order. We each hastily perused the menu. He chose a prawn starter and Majorcan lamb chops. I chose a ceviche to start and followed as my main course with another appetizer of Pata Negra ham and a side order of croquetas, which contained a sharper Spanish cheese. Georj offered to buy a bottle of wine and suggested a Catalonian Priorat, a heavy red from old vines grown on dangerously steep slopes.

After he had placed the order for the wine, he turned back to me. "Do you know Spanish wines?"

"A few," I replied. "I know the French wines better, but I've come to appreciate the Spanish wines more over the past several years. They weren't as available in the States as the French wines were for a long time."

"No, I suspect not. But, tell me, how did you come to have this interest in Islamic culture and the Moors? I doubt that this is taught in your schools in the US."

"Certainly not, no. I've always been interested in Mesopotamia, and my interest grew when I learned about the great libraries that once existed in what is now Iraq. The House of Wisdom in Baghdad in the late eighth century, for example."

"I may have heard of it, but I can't say. I know about the library at Alexandria, of course."

"Yes, a fascinating place. Every ship that came into the port had to turn over all its documents for copying. Then it turned out that the documents were copied, and only the copies were sent back; the library kept the originals."

"That fits with my experience of the eastern mind, at least the near eastern."

We had wandered away from his admission very quickly, and I wondered if he regretted bringing up the incident with his uncle.

"Wine and libraries aside," I said, "would you mind telling me a bit more about the death of your uncle? Since you raised the subject. How did you kill him? Why? Where?"

Georj thought for a moment and then spoke. "Yes, I created an obligation on my part by raising the issue. I will explain."

He paused. "I am originally from a small village. A village like all small villages, its people touchingly close in many aspects, touchingly sad in so many others, and, not so touchingly, evil in others. The man that I killed was my uncle, as I have said. He was evil—a bully, a drunk, lazy, probably a low-level criminal. Who knows?

"He was my mother's brother, and I was always fearful of him when I was young. He was always around, a dark menacing presence. He never harmed me. My mother kept him away from her children—I have a brother and a sister. But that's not the important thing. I never suffered directly under his hand. Others did. I will try to explain briefly.

"It took him a long time to find a wife. No one would have him, because he had already, at a young age, developed a reputation for bullying and being ready to fight at any provocation. He drank too much early on, and both the young women and the young men tried to avoid him.

"I don't know if anyone can explain his behavior. It doesn't seem to fit into the typical generational cycle of domestic problems. My mother, his sister, was a kind and decent person. Their father, my grandfather, was a good man, not a strong person, but not deficient in any substantial way.

"At any rate, my uncle could not find a wife, but finally there was a wedding and a poor girl—she really was just a girl about my age—from a farm in the area, ended up as his wife. I still don't know how that was arranged. My father might have been involved, but I don't like thinking that. My mother never spoke of it. But I always wondered if my uncle might have bought the poor girl."

"Jeez," I said, "this sounds like something out of the Middle Ages."

"Not far off. Some of these old villages can be that way. At any rate, it was a long time before they had any children, but finally his wife had a girl, and then two years later, another. My mother hinted at several miscarriages, but that's not the sort of thing mothers in my village talked to sons about.

"It was well known in the village that he beat his wife, but no one would speak about that either. And the woman's father was too timid or too uncaring to become involved. I mean, after all, if he did sell his daughter to my uncle, what does that tell you?

"My mother did talk to us about her brother's behavior, but she also feared him, and there was nothing she could do."

"Where was your father in all this, if I can ask?" I interrupted.

"Oh, I should have mentioned, he was killed in the war. In *a* war, let me put it that way.

"He was too old to have been there, but he went."

"So, your father was no longer around, and you have an abusive uncle who beats his wife, and no one makes him answer for it, but you one day decide to just kill him?"

"No, of course not. This is why it is good to tell the story and put things in order. You know, like putting the books on the shelf alphabetically or by author, or some such."

"A bit more momentous and consequential, but I'm listening."

"Yes. You see, I mentioned that there were two girls, the two girls who were born after some time to my uncle and his wife. The poor wife was not very pretty. I suppose she could have been, but misery and abuse can make you ugly, I think, or at least render you unattractive. And her life had probably been miserable from an early age. At any rate, the two girls were beautiful, and it was almost as if my uncle had a love-hate relationship with such beautiful creatures around, as if he blamed them for the unattractiveness of his wife. As if there was a cause and effect.

"And interestingly, I don't know where she found the strength, maybe she wanted to protect the girls, I'll never know, but his wife began to stand up for herself a bit. And the price for that was that he beat her more often and more violently than he had before the girls were born."

"And there was no law against this, no way to stop him?"

"Ha, you can't do that even in a society with strong laws and good policing. Where I come from it is barely a concept. No, there is no protection for women."

"So how did you come to the events of two days ago? You don't live in this village any longer, surely."

"No, I should have said," he replied. "I haven't lived there since I finished secondary school, but I visit at least four times a year. I was always informed as to what was going on and talked to my mother regularly on the phone.

"But I'm not making myself clear. The two girls were much younger than me. In fact, their mother was not much older than I am."

"You said *was*, not is."

"Yes, he eventually beat my aunt to death."

"Seriously?"

"Seriously."

"When?"

"About six months ago."

"And he wasn't arrested?"

"No. He claimed she fell down the stairs, but everyone knew."

"Is this the source of the regret you mentioned? That you didn't prevent this?"

At this point the waiter brought our appetizers, and Georj ordered a glass of Albariño to go with his prawns.

"You have listened well," he said, when the waiter departed. "Yes, that is the source of my regret. Or most of it."

"What caused you to decide to do something about him?" I asked.

"What a nice euphemism, 'do something about him.' You mean to rid the earth of his presence? Shoot his miserable ass, as Americans might say?"

I smiled in spite of myself. "Yes, that's my question."

"Let me continue the story after we eat a bit. The prawns are excellent here, as I'm sure you know. And the ceviche which you have ordered is excellent as well. But it is difficult to eat badly in Barcelona. Or in most of Spain, if I'm honest."

We were quiet for a few minutes as we ate. The ceviche was nicely balanced, chilled perfectly and with a touch of spice. There was a small basket of rustic Spanish bread on the table and a slightly grassy olive oil for dipping. I used a small piece of the bread to coax the last bit of ceviche onto the spoon, drizzled a drop or two of oil onto the bread before eating it. A waiter appeared and cleared the dishes and brought new utensils for the next course.

He also brought the Priorat and opened it, and Georj tasted it and told the waiter he could go ahead and pour it.

"Back to my uncle. I have no regrets about killing him, only that I wish I had done it a long time ago, as I said. And please don't misunderstand me, this was not some family honor killing or some stupid peasant vengeance. There is one thing that troubles me, though, and it has to do with beauty and the power of beauty to drive emotions. I will explain.

"I have told you that my uncle's wife, my aunt by marriage, was not a particularly pretty woman. And while we all felt bad for her— by all I mean the family and the community—no one was willing to intervene in any meaningful way. That's usually the case. But as the daughters matured and were reaching puberty, it was becoming obvious that my uncle was beginning to take an unbefitting interest in them, that he was touching them even in public in ways that portended sexual abuse in the near future if it had not yet begun. For my part, I don't think it had. The girls seemed happy and as well-adjusted as one could be in that sort of family. They spent time with my mother, their aunt, and their own mother had treated them well when she was living."

"But you sensed that they were in danger."

"Yes, and here is the thing that causes me shame. I realized that I could not stand the thought of that man ruining those beautiful girls. I remember the day, it was on my last visit before this last, and I actually shuddered at the enormity of what I was thinking. That I had not been willing to protect my aunt, but I knew with all the certainty in the world that I was capable of, and was going to, protect the two girls."

He was silent and looked at me and then took a thoughtful sip of the red wine.

"But isn't it natural to want to protect the young, the innocent? Wasn't that what drove you?"

"I want to think that is the case, but I feel there is more. Although it was too late for my aunt, I tried to discover through research why I was making this distinction between the young women and their mother. I read that humans' fascination with facial beauty may have a strong biological basis, and the preference for attractive faces is already present at birth. Darwin would say it's all about evolution and making choices when it comes to mating and reproducing. I did not like what I was learning about myself, which made me feel I shared some of the father's most loathsome qualities. But I remained resolved that my nieces would not meet the same fate as their mother and that I had made the right decision. There is a line from the English poet, Keats, about the relationship between truth and beauty, and I think about that now, thought about it before I killed him."

"You said that you killed him two days ago. How were you not discovered? Won't you be suspected? How did you kill him?" My mind seemed to want to go to details and not concentrate on the separate moral question of killing to protect beauty. I would have to think about that for a long time.

"I took him to a lake in the area, and I shot him in the head."

"Good lord, just like that?"

"No, not just like that. I said that this was not a crime of passion, but in truth it was a crime of cold passion and complete intent. I planned it carefully. I didn't want to get caught. I don't plan to get caught. I have said he was a drunk, and that made it easy for me to coax him into a car to take him for a drink. I took him late at night to a spot by a lake that we all used to swim in and poured him vodka until he could barely walk. I had developed a scenario in my head of taking him out into the middle of the lake for a swim, something we used to do, and just leaving him there to drown. But I felt that was too cowardly on my part. I felt sick after I played out how it might take place and end. I wanted to tell him what I was going to do and then do it. Then I would feel right about it."

"He never suspected you were up to something?"

"He might have near the end. I told him that I was quite fond of his daughters and offhandedly complimented them. I told him a bit of a story about how such girls needed to be protected and that I felt a certain responsibility to them. It wasn't registering with him, until I said that anyone who would harm girls and women did not deserve to live, and he looked at me with a slightly suspicious look, but then passed it off as a joke. Then I said, 'I plan to kill you in a few minutes.' and I think he began to see that it was real. But he was quite drunk and still not fully comprehending me. I didn't want to prolong it, so I said, 'I have to be leaving soon. I want you to know I am killing you for all your evil, for your poor wife, and to protect your daughters.' I took out the pistol and grabbed him by the hair and turned his head before he could react, and shot him twice at the base of the skull. It is an instant and clean method."

"And you do feel right about it." I said this as a statement, not a question.

"Yes, except for my earlier caveats, I do."

"What will happen with the girls? Now they have neither a father nor a mother?"

"My mother will take them in and raise them. She was already doing that in some ways beforehand."

"I assume you have heard from your mother or someone in the family about his death?"

"Oh yes, the next morning when his body was found. It is being suggested that he had cheated someone dealing in drugs or some other low-life thing and was shot by a gang."

"That's convenient for you. Are there other relatives who might want retribution for this?"

"I don't know who they would be. He was my mom's brother and was always a problem. His father couldn't handle him from an early age. And as I said, I hope my father had nothing to do with setting up the marriage to that poor farm girl."

The waiter had returned with our main courses, and we both focused on eating for a few minutes. The wine went well with the carpaccio and the croquetas. It was a light dinner for me, but I had eaten a late lunch, and this was a good set of choices. Georj was pleased with his lamb and noted how well the wine brought out the flavors of the meat.

As I finished the last of the croquetas, I found myself reflecting on the fact that I had just heard the confession of a killing and had gone ahead and eaten a normal evening meal as if what I had just heard was nothing more than a synopsis from a book or a short story.

I had finished my meal, but Georj was taking longer since his meal was larger. I wiped my mouth and took another sip of the wine.

"I was just wondering as I ate," I said, "how you knew about this way of killing someone, how you were apparently able to do it so effortlessly. Were you in the military?"

He motioned for me to wait. He finished chewing a bite of lamb and wiped his mouth with a napkin and took a small sip of the Priorat. "That method of killing is not really normally used in the military. It is more of a gangster type of execution called a double tap. Two quick shots to the head just below the base of the skull. You can use a small caliber bullet, and it doesn't make too much of a mess. But yes, I was in the military after school, and while I learned conventional methods of fighting, I also learned about this method. I had never done something like that though."

"But had you killed before? I apologize for asking, but I think I would find it impossible to do that even if I felt it was justified."

"I'd rather not talk about my military experiences, but in this case, I was comfortable doing what I did. Many of my fellow countrymen would not have a difficulty doing it. Unlike in your country where madmen go into schools or clubs shooting semi-automatic weapons and then kill themselves. Supreme acts of cowardice. I suspect none of them could do what I did. There is no comparison and probably little frame of reference for you."

"I see. Yes, you are right. I don't have a frame of reference."

"I've spent some time in the States; it is an interesting place. You have a strange kind of violence there. So random, so impersonal in so many ways at one end of the spectrum and intensely personal at the other end. In my country violence is almost always personal and much more predictable. No random shootings.

"You Americans like to think of yourselves as good people, superior to most of the rest of us. Economically I suppose you are the best, or close to, or maybe have been. But I think you are quite naïve in your judgements about human nature."

"Really, what do you mean? You just shot someone without him getting tried in a court and found guilty. Even if he *had* been tried, he wouldn't have received the death penalty, I assume. Are you saying that's a superior approach to a legal system and a police force?"

"You misunderstand me. I'm speaking in general terms. I think that your average citizen still thinks that your society is bound by some religious principles and a golden rule, and that God really does exist and has a kind eye for the United States. And you are still surprised when a gunman kills a bunch of school kids or concert goers or whomever. And you are so convinced that it was just another mental aberration that you never make any legal changes to control the weapons. You just won't admit that human nature is not that good to begin with."

"I'm not sure the thinking is that deep. I think it's more a fetish. Built on a cowboy and wild west myth."

He pursed his lips and looked at me intently for a few moments before responding.

"I didn't mean to be personally insulting when I mentioned naiveté a moment ago," he said. "But what you have just said about the cowboys and this fetish—doesn't that support my argument?"

"I suppose so, but it seems to me we have wandered away from the original story, which is your personal one. Are you saying that because your society is used to personal and, by some suggested implication, justified violence, that your deed is morally acceptable? I see some measure of justice in what you did, assuming you had the facts right, but it is anarchic and dangerous as a model."

"Let me come at this from a different direction. Would I be correct in assuming that you, yourself, have always lived a pretty safe and protected life? Have you ever been attacked or feared for your personal safety? Has your family always been safe?"

I was a bit surprised at this tack and thought about it for a moment.

"Yes, I have had a very safe existence so far. Or at least a fortunate one. And no one in my family has suffered from violence."

"So, your frame of reference is always going to be different from mine. I said earlier that this action on my part was not part of a peasant honor killing. But there is a history of that, and of cultural and religious differences that have led to great excesses in my country. You've never seen that. It is not a part of your culture to think in these terms. Your civil war was a long time ago, and while your country is still quite divided, it seems, on lots of cultural issues, you are unlikely to have another war any time soon. I could not say that about my own."

"I'm still having trouble making the connection."

"I will try to tie it together in one final argument. We have two types of killing in our country. One is deeply personal, like what I just did. The second is ethnically or culturally driven and with long historical roots, almost always. Think of it as an ongoing social motif. It is in the air. You breathe it and think it and wonder when it will happen again. Because it will.

"In your country, you have many murders, mainly in poorer areas it seems, and some of that is personal, I'm sure, but lots seem to be gang or drug related and such. But on the national level, you don't have to worry about the Mormons, say, or the former southern states, suddenly deciding to secede or to begin bombings or random acts of violence. Thus, you create this fantasy set of circumstances, and everyone buys semi-automatic rifles and lots of ammunition and pretends that you are living on a lawless frontier that hasn't existed for over a century. I know a bit about your history. And to me, that fantasy creates a moral vacuum that generates the senseless random killings that would never happen where I am from.

"What I did is not justifiable in your country or in mine, really, but I just protected two young women from probable rape and continued abuse, and possibly ruined lives. And what I took away did not diminish our society. I will trade that for your system."

I realized that I had no argument that could challenge what Georj had said. Or none that he would accept. For him, the killing was a moral and morally justified act, and he was not expanding the concept to its logical conclusion of rampant lawlessness. He had spoken of the imaginary lawless American frontier while he practiced a version of that kind of justice in his own country.

The waiter arrived to clear the plates and to ask if we wanted one of the four desserts he listed for us. I chose a poached pear tart with a sherry glaze, and he chose a slice of lemon-infused local cake. I ordered a white dessert wine that reminded me of the Italian Vin Santo, and he ordered a light sherry that I had found too sweet in the past.

"I apologize for ruining your evening with such a sordid story," he said to me. "Let me make slight amends by buying your dinner, if I could."

"No, this has been fascinating and illuminating," I said in reply. "You have given me something to think about. Cultural underpinnings and history are so critical to how a society behaves. I will bear in mind what you told me this evening as I think about the influence of Islam, the arrival of the North Africans in Spain, and the life of that Moorish period here. And the intolerance that followed. I don't know if there is a lesson there or not."

Our desserts and wines arrived, and we turned to a discussion of the various dessert wines available around the world.